TOWARD
THEOLOGY

Jerry H. Gill
**Professor of Philosophy
and Religion
Eastern College**

UNIVERSITY
PRESS OF
AMERICA

LANHAM • NEW YORK • LONDON

Copyright © 1982 by

University Press of America,™ Inc.

4720 Boston Way
Lanham, MD 20706

3 Henrietta Street
London WC2E 8LU England

Library of Congress Cataloging in Publication Data

Gill, Jerry H.
    Toward theology.

    1. Theology, Doctrinal. I. Title.
BT75.2.G55   230   82–45009
ISBN 0–8191–2429–X   AACR2
ISBN 0–8191–2430–3 (pbk.)

for

My Sisters and Brothers

at

Central Baptist Church

Table of Contents

Introduction

The Place of Theology

Religion may be thought of as providing four dimensions of meaning, or expressing itself in four modes. At its heart religion is (1) a deep personal experience, an existential encounter. This encounter takes place within (2) the context of an historical and social community and carries with it (3) some form of ethical imperative. Finally, religious experience (4) seeks an over-arching system of thought which explores and clarifies its own meaning. This latter characteristic is usually given the title "theology", and has always played a crucial role in the Christian religion.

While it is no substitute for the experiential dimension of Christian religious awareness, the development of a thorough and consistent way of thinking and speaking about that awareness is nonetheless an important task. For not only is it confusing and counter-productive to ignore doing theology, it is essentially impossible, since to seek to do so is itself a theological posture. Moreover, our initial religious awareness, as well as our day-by-day experience, does not take place in a theological vacuum. To a large extent the very character of our religious encounter itself is a function of the particular theologies we hold, whether tacitly or explicitly.

Since we cannot avoid theologizing, we should seek to do the best job we can, knowing full-well that we shall never complete the task. For not only is God beyond our full understanding, but we ourselves are continually changing, both as individuals and as a society. The title of this book,

"Toware Theology", is meant to serve as a reminder of these two important points. We are always and only moving _toward_ a full understanding of our interaction _with_ God. Even if we believe that God initiates our religious knowledge, it still must become _our_ knowledge, and this very belief itself flows from a theological posture. In the final analysis theology is a _human_ enterprise, and this truth both challenges us to engage in it and cautions us to do so humbly.

Traditionally theology is approached in one of three ways: either historically, biblically, or systematically. The first half of this book offers an introductory survey of systematic theology. Only major themes are treated, with crucial issues and positions being sketched out. In addition to providing an outline of the different postures taken by Christian thinkers throughout the ages, Part One of the book comprises a backdrop against which the second half will take shape. In Part Two I shall try to provide some fresh insights into the main issues of Christian theology following what might be termed an "organic", rather than a systematic approach. I employ the term 'organic' at this juncture in order to distinguish the approach I am proposing from a strictly "logical" approach. An organic exploration is more related to biology than it is to logic. The point is to establish a perspective which views theological themes as related as the members and systems of a cellular body are related - functionally and symbiotically.

The image of the hub and spokes of a wheel may prove helpful. The center of Christian experience and thought is Jesus Christ, his incarnation and atonement. The other dimensions of experience and doctrine extend outward from this center toward everyday life itself, represented by the rim of the wheel. Whatever stance we take on whatever theological issues, it must be one which is in line with the central thrust of the incarnation and atonement. Far too often theological thinkers have tried to force Christian thought into a systematic mold, rather than allowing it to flow functionally or organically, in harmony with Christian experience.

Perhaps it should go without saying that the second half of this book is neither offered as the _end_ nor as the _only_ beginning point of Christian theology. It is simply one person's effort at thinking about the main motifs of the Christian Faith. Hopefully it affords some fresh insight into some old themes and serves as a challenge for its readers to set out on their own journey "toward theology". Because the emphasis in this introductory approach is on the individual reader's development of a theology of his or her own, a minimum of historical, and technical names and terms will be employed. Two final words to those embarking on this journey: we must begin where we are and the true goal of the journey is the going itself.

Part One

A

Systematic Survey

Chapter One

The Basis of Christian Authority

When decisions and controversies arise within the lives of individual Christians and the Christian community, some means of settlement must be invoked. The question of what is to serve as the means of settlement is the question of authority. To what do we appeal to settle issues involving Christian practice and thought? It may prove helpful to envision the main answers to this question arrayed along a spectrum, moving from right to left.

The right side of the spectrum is comprised of those Christians who emphasize the necessity of having an infallible and external authority for faith and life. Such views are often termed "objectivist". At the right hand pole is the view that the church serves as the basis of Christian authority. This is the view taken by such groups as Roman Catholics, Eastern Orthodoxy, and the Church of England. For these groups the church is the final interpreter of scripture, experience, and reason.

Two passages of scripture are traditionally employed to substantiate this position. One is Matthew 16: 18-19 wherein Peter is both designated by Jesus as the rock upon which the church was to be built and is given the "keys to the kingdom", to bind and loose as he will. It is argued that Peter was in essence the first Pope, and that he passed this infallible authority within the church to succeeding Popes. This argument is used in modified form by Orthodox and Anglican theologians to apply to the church

1

in general as the final Christian authority.

The second scripture passage referred to is the one wherein Jesus promises that when the Holy Spirit comes He will guide the Apostles into "all truth". The argument here is that even though there well may be disagreement amongst thinkers within the church, the Holy Spirit will so guide their final decisions as to guarantee their correctness. This is said to be the point of Christ's promise, to provide a reliable source of infallible authority for faith and life.

A third line of argument often given for this position is that some form of objective and/ or infallible line of authority is <u>necessary</u> in order to guarantee a continuous connection between God's original revelation and the on-going life of the Christian community. Without such an "external" source of authority each person or local group would be left to decide subjectively for themselves what constitute proper Christian views and practices. It is argued that this would lead to continual conflict, splintering, and loss of effectiveness within the Christian community.

Also aligned along the right side of the continuum are those who take the position that the objective source of authority is the Judeo-Christian scripture. These Christians maintain that in the final analysis it is the scripture which must interpret the church and not <u>vice versa</u>. This view urges that only the scripture can serve as an external and objective authority since it exists apart from the changes and controversies which are inevitable in the church as an institution. Moreover, those who take this view usually maintain that the Christian scriptures are without error, at least with respect to matters of faith and practice if not in every detail.

It should be noted that this interpretation of scripture as an inerrant authority is relatively new in Christian history. It is taken by members of the "fundamentalist" or "evangelical" movements to be the traditionally orthodox position, but there is good evidence to show that not only is it strictly a Protestant phenomenon but it is essentially a Twentieth Century idea. There is no compelling reason to believe that Luther and Calvin, for instance, thought the scriptures to be free of error. In addition, the discovery in recent decades of hundreds of versions of the scriptures, which while only differing from one another slightly nevertheless do differ, has forced those who take this view to maintain that only the original scriptural manuscripts (the "autographs") were inerrant.

The lines of support for the position which takes the scripture as an infallible authority are drawn primarily from the scripture itself. There are numerous passages throughout the Old Testament wherein it is claimed that the "Word of the Lord" is always correct, effective, and final. Likewise, Jesus frequently claims that "the scripture cannot be broken" and that "not one jot or tittle shall pass away" (Matt. 5:18). Moreover, Paul explicitly says that "All scripture is inspired by God and is profitable...(2 Tim. 3:16). The Greek word translated "inspired" in this passage literally means "God-breathed". Thus it is claimed that the scripture must be infallible since it is breathed by God's own Spirit. It should be noted that those who hold this view do not maintain that the original manuscripts of the scripture were "dictated" by God, but only that the Holy Spirit so guided the authors as to keep them free from error.

The other main line of support offered for this position is similar to one mentioned in connection with the previous position, namely the

3

argument from necessity. It is claimed that without an inerrant scriptural authority we would be left to our own "subjective" devices in deciding questions of faith and practice. Not only would this lead to chaos in the Christian community, but it would be tantamount to placing ourselves above God's word, since we would interpret and judge it by our own ideas. Moreover, it would seem inappropriate for God to go to all the trouble of revealing the truth to humankind and then fail to provide an objective, inerrant source of authority for interpreting that revelation. Thus it is claimed that the scriptures are without error, since an infallible authority is necessary to the life of the Christian community.

Before turning to a consideration of those positions on the left side of our spectrum, I should like to review a few of the more serious difficulties that can be raised with regard to the views discussed thus far. To begin with, the argument from necessity is not very convincing. In addition to the fact that there are many things which seem "necessary" but which do not exist (e.g. International Law), neither the church nor the scripture has provided an infallible guide down through Christian history. The Popes and high church councils have disagreed with one another, and all of the original biblical manuscripts were lost very early in Christian history. Until the Twentieth Century we had only about a half dozen copies of the scripture and now we have hundreds. Although they mostly differ in nonessentials, there are certain basic differences, and in any case the idea of inerrancy seems inapplicable. Since the Christian community has existed all these centuries--and God has been active in it--without an infallible authority, it hardly seems that such an authority could be necessary.

Secondly, even if one were to grant that either the Church or the scripture is infallible, we are still left with the task of properly interpreting what these authorities mean. No utterances or teachings are beyond interpretation, and those of the Church and the scripture are perhaps especially difficult to interpret, if the controversies of history are anything to go by. Thus it can be asked, in a kind of reductio ad absurdum move, why would God go to all the trouble to provide an infallible source of authority and yet leave us with only fallible means of interpreting it? There seems to be no escape from the human responsibility of the Christian community in questions of authority.

Finally, it can be objected that the appeal to scripture in order to substantiate the authority of scripture, in addition to being circular, is also guilty of faulty exegesis. For it can be shown that most of the biblical references to the "Word of God", whether in the Old or New Testaments, are not to any written documents at all but refer to God's self revelation in history and experience. The Old and New Testaments did not become "Scripture" as we know it until several hundred years after the events they describe. Even Paul's statement in 2 Timothy 3:16 cannot be taken to refer to any part of the New Testament. Moreover, Jesus' references to the Old Testament sometimes draw directly on the Apocrypha (which are excluded from the scripture by those who urge biblical inerrancy) and frequently they refer to the Greek translation of the Old Testament. In fact, Paul's reference to scripture as "God-breathed" is in connection with those scriptures which made Timothy "wise unto salvation", namely copies of Greek translations of the Old Testament (cf. 2 Timothy 3:15). So it would seem that whatever view we take of the authority of the scripture, it must be broad enough to include translations and copies--and this would seem to exclude the notion of inerrancy.

On the left-side of our original continuum stand those Christians who empahsize more personal, flexible, and "subjective" criteria of authority. At the polar end of this side of the spectrum are those who find the source of authority in the rational processes of the individual believer. According to this view each person must, in the final analysis, decide for themselves what is correct belief and/or practice. Only by trusting their own reason can a person protect the sanctity of individual faith. At the everyday level this is in fact what people do; at a deeper level, even if a person submits to the authority of the church or the scripture, that person decides that this is the reasonable thing to do.

Although the authority of reason was given a high place in Medieval Christianity--it was generally held that by reason alone a person could establish that God is, but not Who he is--it was not until the Enlightenment that reason came into its own as a source of authority in Christian theology. By the 19th century the dominant posture in Christendom was that of accommodating theology to the dictates of Rationalism. This trend reached its peak at the turn of the century in the theological movement known as Liberalism, which emphasized a rational investigation of the scripture, the social implications of the Gospel, and the similarity between Christianity and other world religions.

There are two main lines of argument used to substantiate this trust in reason as the final authority in theology. The first is based on the concept of the image of God in humankind. Since our natural rational capacities are given by God in creation, it is not only appropriate but imperative that we use them in matters of faith and life. One of God's chief characteristics is reason, and since we are created in his image we too ought to be characterized by rational behavior. Moreover, throughout the scripture we are urged to "try the spirits" and to be able to "give a reason" for the hope that is within us.

The second line of argument flows from the modern concern to avoid the evils of traditionalism and authoritarianism in theological matters. The main emphasis here is on all the atrocities and exploitations which have been perpetrated in the name of God by those who hide behind the church and/or scripture for their authority. It is maintained that the only way to emancipate ourselves from theological "big-brotherism" and to guarantee against spiritual exploitation is to rely upon individual reason as the means of discerning religious truth from error.

A final main position on authority is that which stresses the ultimate importance of personal experience or the "inner voice" of God's spirit. There are two main brands of this "experiential" approach to theological authority. One is that of spiritualist or holiness movements and the others is that of the Christian existentialists. The former focus on the inner-guidance of the Holy Spirit, in conjunction with the scripture, while the latter emphasize the necessity of each individual's choice on the basis of their own self-understanding.

In support of the inner-guidance posture the scriptural promises concerning "the spirit of Christ who will lead you to the truth" are invoked, as are the examples of the patriarchs, prophets, apostles, and Jesus himself. The existentialist posture is supported by the argument that in the final analysis all persons must and

7

do decide for themselves, not on the basis of reason (which is always very limited) but on the basis of volitional faith alone. It is also claimed that such commitment is the only means of insuring authenticity in spiritual matters. Soren Kierkegaard is usually interpreted as being the "father" of this point of view. Both of these postures share in the conviction that books and institutions, even the scripture and the church, are dead apart from the personal or spiritual quality of individual experience--and both are distrustful of reason, the main form of human pride.

In concluding this chapter let me point out some of the criticisms that can be raised against the positions on the left-side of our continuum. First off, it can be argued that both reason and experience are insufficient as sources of authority in and of themselves because they fail to fulfill one of the main requirements of authority, namely that of bringing about unity and agreement within the Christian community. The inherent individualism in these postures leads, rather, to increased disagreements and divisions in the community, as the fantastic number of Protestant sects clearly indicates. These positions are simply too subjective.

A second and related criticism pertains to the anti-historical and anti-social character of the approach on the left-side of the continuum. Not only do they not emphasize the continuity of faith between and among believers of every age and the dialogical quality of faith in community, but they actually stand opposed to these all-important considerations. Here again these positions reveal themselves to be too individualistic. The Judeo-Christian faith is deeply historical and communal, and thus its source of authority must be more broadly based than either of these approaches will allow.

8

These, then, are the main positions along the continuum representing approaches to the question of authority in the Christian Faith. Each has its strengths, and each its weaknesses. It should be clear that no position answers all the questions, on this issue or any other issue. Nevertheless, some positions are more responsible than others. We shall return to the question of authority toward the end of Part Two.

Chapter Two

The Nature of God

Most systematic theologies devote a good deal of space to explicating the various attributes of God, such as spirituality, wisdom, power, love, etc. In a short book such as this we can only choose one key theme by way of introducing some of the various issues and positions involved in dealing with the Christian understanding of the character of God.

One central theme is that of the nature of God's sovereign power. In what sense is God in control of the universe, especially with regard to the lives and destinies of human beings? Traditionally this question has often been put in the form of a dilemma called "the problem of evil": if God is all-powerful and all-loving, then evil should not exist; but evil exists, therefore God is either not all-powerful or not all-loving. Either God wishes to eliminate evil and cannot, in which case God is not all-powerful, or God could eliminate evil but will not, in which case God is not all-loving.

There are two main approaches to this dilemma within Christian theology, each of which can be sub-divided into two somewhat distinct postures. We shall look at each of these approaches in turn.

The first main approach can be termed Monism, for it emphasizes the absolute and comprehensive character of divine power in the universe; God's will is the only will that ultimately counts in the course of events. The unqualified version of Monism may be found in one of two common forms.

11

One form simply denies the existence of evil; it maintains that evil is unreal. In its extreme form this is the posture taken by the Christian Scientist Church. A more common and traditionally orthodox form is the one advocated by Augustine when he argued that evil is simply the absence or "privation" of good, that evil has no positive existence of its own. Thus unqualified Monism solves the problem of evil by affirming God's absolute sovereignty and denying the ultimate reality of evil.

The qualified version of Monism, that expressed by Calvin and most theologians of the Reformation tradition, makes a distinction between the directive and the permissive will of God. The former is said to represent God's long-range purpose for persons and nations, while the latter represents divine short-term allowances for the contingencies of historical and social circumstances. Thus evil is said to exist within God's permissive will without in any way being in conflict with God's directive will. Another tack often made within the posture I am calling qualified Monism is the one which maintains that whatever appears to be evil from our human perspective is actually an important part of God's overall plan and is necessary to its fulfillment. Evil is allowed to exist because it provides a "proving ground" for the development of spiritual maturity.

The substantiation given for Monism is usually three-fold. To begin with, it is argued that the scripture clearly teaches that God is in complete control of the cosmos. From the first chapter of Genesis on through the last chapter of Revelation God is portrayed as the creator and sustainer of the universe, as well as the initiator and final arbiter of human history and destiny. To theologians within the Reformed tradition, such as and most especially Calvin, the absolute sovereignty of God is the most important scriptural doctrine, all else follows from it.

Another line of argument used to substantiate the Monist position stems from the belief in God's final victory. If one believes that the ultimate triumph of good, the fulfillment of God's will, must take place, then one must believe that God is in absolute control. It is maintained that a strong doctrine of sovereignty, such as with Monism, is necessary to guarantee the final victory of the forces of good. Anything short of such a strong position carries with it the possibility that good and God's will may not prevail.

A third and more philosophical supportive move focuses on the meaning of the concept of God. It is urged that the very notion of "God" entails complete sovereignty and thus a strong Monistic doctrine. For there to be any way in which God could be limited, by other forces of human decisions, would be contradictory. God means, by definition, that being who creates, sustains, and controls the universe. To speak of a being who is less than this is not to speak of God at all, but of some other, lesser being. Because it parallels Anselm's famous argument for God's existence, this move might be termed "the ontological proof" of God's sovereignty.

There are, to be sure, certain difficulties which some Christian thinkers find with the Monistic position, both at the scriptural and at the experiential level. These difficulties center around Monism's failure to take human struggle and choice seriously enough. The human encounter with evil and suffering is far too real and important to be dealt with by some abstract reasoning process which reduces it to a mere "appearance" or "the absence of good". To treat the suffering of innocent people, especially children, and the prospering of the wicked in terms of a "lack of the divine perspective" is to make a mockery of both God and humankind. The same holds true for the decision making process. If the choices we make, especially those pertaining to our relation to God, are not real and binding on God

as well as ourselves, then the whole human drama
is nothing but a divine and sadistic puppet-show.

These same arguments can be given a scriptural
basis. The dynamic dialogue of the Old Testament
between Jehovah and the children of Israel, the
constant urgings and warnings given to the people
to choose to follow the Lord's way, and the "bar-
gaining" with God engaged in by Abraham, Moses,
David, and the prophets all imply that human suffering and struggle are every bit as real as God's
sovereignty. Moreover, the central thrust of the
New Testament toward the cultivation of belief, to
say nothing of Christ's own struggle and suffering,
clearly presupposes that evil and choice are to be
taken more seriously than any form of Monism allows.

Over against Monism stands various varieties
of Dualism, the position that maintains there are
two main forces at work in the world, the power of
good and the power of evil, and that these two are
engaged in real and crucial conflict with each
other. In some Eastern religions these two powers
are seen as either equally divine and eternally at
odds, such as in Zoroastrianism, or as dialectically
complementary to each other, as with the Yin and
Yang principles of Buddhism. These postures might
be termed unqualified dualism, and parallels are
difficult to find in the Christian tradition.

One Christian interpretation which might be
thought of as a form of unqualified dualism is
that which posits, in addition to a creative, all-
powerful God, certain fundamental structures which
provide the context within which God must work.
According to this position, the ontological structure of reality is an eternally given, it was not
created nor is it a being of any kind. Rather it
is the framework within which reality takes place.
God too works within this framework, the divine
creative powers being shaped by, and thus in some
sense limited by, this primordial structure. This

does not constitute a substantive limitation in the usual sense, but is rather a formal characteristic, much as in the commonly accepted notion that it does not detract from God's power to say that he is unable to do something logically self-contradictory. (e.g. make a rock so big that God cannot lift it).

Another way to give this dualistic position a Christian interpretation is to express it in terms of the relationship between the principles of creativity and discreativity. Thus within the given primordial framework, God initiates creative power. However, as with our own physical reality, the given structure provides a certain amount of "inertia" or drag which must continually be overcome and/or planned against or else creative efforts either will never get off the ground or will collapse as a result of entropy. This "cosmic gravity" or "ontological entropy" works as a principle of discreativity against God's creative activity eternally; it can never be overcome finally, because it is a necessary condition of there being any activity at all. Nevertheless, because of the creative and living character of God we can rely on the triumph of good in the sense that discreativity can be kept at bay. It can even be "recycled" to serve good ends, in the same way the pull of gravity is used to overcome itself when stones are placed on top of one another in the building up of a stone wall.

Along with these various forms of unqualified dualism there are at least two varieties of qualified dualism. One is that position which posits a finite, growing God. The idea here is that although there are various difficulties and negative powers which cause all evil in the world, and although God does not as yet have these under divine control, God is struggling to do so, and because of the quality of divine character we can be confident that God will eventually be victorious.

Moreover, this victory will be hastened by the active co-operation of Christians who are committed to God's will. One strength of this position lies in its insight that it is not necessary to think of God as a <u>static</u> being, one who has and will always be the same. Another is that it prefers giving up on the omnipotence of God, at least temporarily, to giving up on God's loving character in order to deal with the dilemma of the problem of evil. This position has not been widely accepted in Christian circles, primarily because it seems difficult to reconcile with scripture.

A final view, also a form of qualified dualism, is the one which affirms the notion of God's <u>self-limitation</u>. The argument runs like this. Prior to the creation of human beings God could be characterized as completely sovereign, at least in the sense admitted by those who propose a primordial structure co-terminus with God. However, once having chosen to create other beings with independent volitional capacities, God thereby set aside complete autonomy and control. This choice constitutes a self-limitation on God's behalf, one that divinity imposed on itself in order to achieve a higher goal than simple sovereignty. The higher goal was the existence of volitional beings who could enter into dialogical relationship with one another and with God. An analogy might be drawn from the sort of self-limitation accepted by parents when they choose to have children. It is their sovereign choice, but once the child is on the scene there are inevitable conflicts of will.

Another way to develop this position is in terms of the concept of personhood. If humans are to be thought of as persons, then choice is necessary to their nature. Choice, in turn, necessitates the possibility of error and/or evil, and given the number of choices demanded in life, possibility flows naturally into actuality. Perhaps the paradigm for this logic can be found in the person of Christ, who is said to have been confronted and "tempted like as we" yet chose not to sin. For this to have been a real choice the possibility of Christ's disobedience must also have been real. And such a possibility can helpfully be described as a risk resulting from God's self-imposed limitation.

The immediately foregoing argument points the way to the sort of scriptural support which can be given for a qualified dualistic interpretation of God's sovereignty. The biblical emphasis on God's love and powers of persuasion, as contrasted to powers of coercion, would seem to render some form of qualification of the absolute notion of sovereignty not only viable but necessary Throughout both Testaments God never forces someone to do anything against their will; rather God offers, urges, scolds, warns, and cajoles persons and nations toward the fulfillment of divine purposes. Moses' difficulties with Israel, the prophets' messages to the kings, and Peter's acceptance of Gentile Christians (Acts 9-15) come readil; to mind. Moreover, the gospel itself is offered and must be received, it is not thrust upon persons unilaterally. And people are allowed to choose the wrong path, to do evil, and to say "No!" to God.

There are two main criticisms of the various forms of dualism which bear mentioning. The first pertains to the question of the ultimate victory of God and the powers of good. If there are any possible limitations to God's sovereignty, it is claimed, then there is no guarantee that divine purposes will prevail. If the forces of evil are not in principle under divine control or if humans can say "No!" to God, then there is no assurance that good shall conquer evil. Moreover, it may be urged, the very notion of limitation, even if self-imposed, is at odds with both the concept and the character of God.

17

Secondly, it can be argued that even though various forms of qualified dualism may account for <u>moral</u> evil ("man's inhumanity to man"), they do not account for <u>natural</u> evil (famine, earthquake, pestilence, etc.). One would think that no matter what the limitations of creating real persons, God could have built a world free of the upheavals of nature in which millions are killed yearly. This criticism comes, of course, from those who are equally dissatisfied with monistic interpretations of sovereignty and the problem of evil. The rejoinder is usually made that <u>any</u> non-static structure whatsoever must necessar<u>il</u>y have certain processes in it which will at times bring difficulty and grief to those living in it. But this is not the place to begin a whole new round of discussion. We shall return to this issue in Chapter Eleven.

Chapter Three

Human Nature

There are three central issues pertaining to the Christian view of humankind which bear special attention in an introductory theological survey. One has to do with whether or not humans have freedom, and this issue is closely linked to the preceding discussion of the sovereignty of God. Another involves the question of the basic moral quality of humans, whether they are essentially "good" or essentially "evil". This question is usually posed in relation to the notion of original sin. A third issue is that of the relation of soul and body in the Christian conception of personhood. I shall deal with these issues in the order mentioned, and as fairly as possible in the space available. The natural connections among the issues should surface in the process.

The question of human freedom, closely tied as it is to the question of God's sovereignty, tends to revolve around two main points of view. On the one side is the Reformed or Calvinistic tradition, emphasizing the unconditional election and irresistible grace. On the other side is the Arminian or Anabaptist tradition, emphasizing conditional election and limited but real freedom. The former view is a corollary of stressing the absolute sovereignty of God, while the latter is a corollary of the notion of self-limitation.

Unconditional election refers to the idea that in choosing those persons who will participate in salvation--as well as those who will not--God does not rely on whether or not those persons have or have not done this or that. Rather, God is said to exercise sovereign control irrespective of the various differences between and among people. In other words, there are no conditions which determine God's election, no prerequisites that people can or must meet in order to be elected. God simply chooses some to be saved, quite apart from any considerations of merit of faith. In fact, election is itself viewed here as a precondition of having faith, and not vice versa. In like fashion, once God has chosen a particular person this grace cannot be resisted; election is a gift which must be received. Otherwise divine choices would not be final, and God would not be sovereign.

Support for this point of view is drawn from two primary sources, the scripture and the implications of the systematic approach to theology. In the Old Testament those who defy God's will, such as the pharoah in Exodus, are frequently described as having had their "hearts hardened by God." In the New Testament Jesus asserts that no person can come to him unless he is drawn by the Father and Paul stresses that those who are in Christ were chosen "before the foundations of the world." Moreover, if one is going to do justice to a strong notion of sovereignty, election and grace cannot be thought of as conditional and/or optional. If human merit and/or choice figure into the picture, election and grace, and ultimately sovereignty itself, lose their meaning.

The sorts of objections which can be and have been raised in opposition to this view lead directly to the Arminian or Anabaptist position. Here election is seen as hinging on the response of the individual person to God's love and forgiveness. It is said to be a "class" concept in that God is viewed as electing all those (the class of) persons who accept the gospel. In the same way, grace, to be grace, must not only be freely given, it must be subject to rejection as well; otherwise it is coersive. As Jacob Arminius put it, while one certainly does not praise a beggar for receiving a gift from the king, it goes without saying that a gift is not a gift unless it is received. The notion of a gift carries with it the idea of reception and thus logically implies the possibility of rejection as well. The beggar <u>could</u>, after all, refuse the gift; otherwise it is not a gift but a law.

Support for this view is once again both scriptural and theological. It is argued that the whole drive of both Testaments is toward the cruciality of human choice of and cooperation with God's purposes, and that in particular the New Testament stresses the benefits of belief and the liabilities of disbelief. To make such conditions irrelevant to election is to reduce the urgency of the Gospel to a mere charade. Moreover, Paul specifically states (Romans 8:29) that God's election is based on his foreknowledge of how individuals would respond to his forgiving love. Theologically, it is maintained that the doctrine of election must be developed in harmony with the teachings and experience of the Gospel and not <u>vice versa</u>. The approach to theology must move <u>inductively</u> from scripture and experience toward doctrine, not deductively from the latter to the former.

To turn to our second main consideration, the question of the moral condition of humanity is quite closely joined to the foregoing discussion. One of the presuppositions of the posture which stresses unconditional election and irresistible grace is that of the <u>total depravity</u> of human nature. Since all humans have sinned, whether on their own or in Adam (or both!), none are worthy of a relationship with God, all deserve death. Because we are all depraved and have had the image of God destroyed in us, our election is strictly an undeserved gift. Furthermore, our depraved condition eliminates the possibility of our refusing God's gracious gift

of election, for the capacity for choice is itself
a function of the image of God. In our sinful
state we can do nothing good, not even receive
grace, unless God chooses to elect us and grant us
the capacity to accept divine love in Christ.

This interpretation of the human condition
draws heavily upon the first few chapters of Genesis and Paul's analysis in the first seven chapters of Romans. In sum, all have sinned, the wages
of sin is death, and all our righteousness is as
filthy rags. Moreover, this interpretation not
only fits with a strong doctrine of sovereignty
and with the "penal satisfaction" view of Christ's
atonement (which we shall discuss in the next
chapter), but it jibes with our personal lives as
well. We all know from experience that "the heart
is deceitfully wicked above all things."

Correspondingly, one of the basic presuppositions of the posture which stresses conditional
election and limited freedom is that humankind is
not totally depraved, but is, rather, only partially depraved. According to this view, the image of
God is not destroyed because of sin, but is severe-
ly distorted. Here it is maintained that there
remains a point of contact between God and humankind, which at the very least consists of the
ability to understand, choose, and receive the
Gospel of God's love. Moreover, while there is
no denying that there is a strong propensity toward evil in all humans, this position also acknowledges the human capacity for both good and
growth. We are, in the vernacular, a "mixed bag"
of positive and negative qualities.

To place this position in relation to the
issue of sovereignty discussed in the preceding
chapter, its proponents would hold that our capacity to choose is a direct result of God's self-
limiting act of creating true persons. The capacity itself is God-given and good, and remains

22

so no matter how it is used--or abused. The effects of our abuse of these God-given capacities
may well "bend" us in the direction of consistently choosing evil, but they do not render the capacities themselves evil, nor do they obliterate them.

Another aspect of the posture presently being
discussed, and indeed of the general issue under
consideration, can be brought out by means of the
distinction between original sin and original
guilt. The view which emphasizes the total depravity of humankind would speak of all persons being
guilty as a result of the original choice of Adam
and Eve. The view stressing partial depravity
would,on the contrary, speak only of original sin
in the sense that although sin may have come into
human existence as a result of some primordial
choice, each individual person is not held accountable for how they respond to the capacities and
propensities which they encounter in their own
existence. Sin is thus thought of as comprising
a very real dimension of our lives, especially
perhaps in our social and cultural relationships,
but each person is only called upon to face and
answer for their own.

A third but closely related major issue in
coming to grips with the Christian view of human
nature is that of the relation between the notions
of body, soul, and personhood. This issue is forcefully focused in the conflict between what might
be termed the "Greek view" and the "Hebrew view."
The former, which has traditionally been the standard position in Christian theology, is essentially dualistic, while the latter, the more biblical
position, is essentially holistic.

The Greek or dualistic view sees a fundamental
antipathy between the body and the soul. The body
is regarded as opposed to the spiritual character
and purpose of the soul, as the seat of all those
forces which draw humans downward, away from their

higher destiny. This position has some basis in the letters of Paul, but essentially came into Christian theology through the writings of Augustine, who was greatly influenced by Neo-Platonism. Plato himself had regarded the body as "the prison house of the soul", and Augustine was a dominant influence on the Reformation. The result has been to view the soul as synonymous with the person, and to regard the body as a necessary but temporary evil.

This dualism leads to an acceptance of the Greek idea of the immortality of the soul. Once again, this is a platonic doctrine which has come to be regarded as an essentially Christian idea. Many theology books and sermons have been developed to explain and substantiate this belief, and if asked most Christians would affirm that they believe in the immortality of the soul. Of course, what is usually meant in these cases is a belief in life after death, but the focus on the soul at this juncture, to the exclusion of the body, is what is crucial.

On the other hand, the Hebrew or holistic view regards the person as synonymous with both the body and the soul, and accordingly does not locate evil and/or sin in the body anymore than in the soul. The body is regarded as a vital part of God's creation and has been sanctified by the Incarnation of the Word into human form. Not only does the Old Testament not make distinctions between souls and bodies, but Jesus himself consistently deals with the whole person in his ministry, and Paul stresses the cruciality of "the resurrection of the body." In fact, the Apostles' Creed itself actually employs this latter phrase, even though many of us may never have thought about its meaning. Thus this position can safely be said to be the more biblical of the two under consideration.

According to this position the body is no less a part of the real person than is the soul; rather, the two arc best regarded as interrelated dimensions of one reality. Furthermore, the Christian notion of life after death is seen to include the body as well as the soul--the whole person is redeemed and resurrected. The paradigm for this resurrection is Jesus' own resurrection, which clearly involved his body. Paul speaks of it as a "spiritual body", one that was and will be recognizable and capable of interaction. More will be said about this in Chapter Ten.

Chapter Four

The Nature of Christ

Down through the ages of Christian thought
the question of the nature of Christ has been
perhaps the most crucial and complex of all theological questions. The focus of this question
has usually been around the sense in which
Christ can be said to be both divine and human.
This focus can, in turn, be said to have three
main facets, namely the nature of Christ's relation to the Creator (and the Holy Spirit; the
Trinity), Character of the dual-nature in the
person of Christ himself, and the way in which
this dual-nature is revealed to and experienced
by humans. We shall trace these three interra-
lated facets in this order.

The different views of Christ's relation
to the Creator can be lined up along a continuum
moving from left to right. At the extreme left
is the view that Christ the Son, along with the
Holy Spirit, is really simply a different mani-
festation of God's being. In this view each person of the Godhead or Trinity is thought of as a
different mode of expression of one and the same
divine being. The strength of this position lies
in its explanation of the unitary character of
the Godhead and its stress on the traditionally
important notion of monotheism. Its weakness
lies in its inability to do justice to the obvious biblical depiction of the distinct wills of
Christ and the Creator, as in the garden scene
when Christ prays, "Not my will but Thine".

At the extreme right of the continuum is the
view asserting that Christ was created by God the
Creator, as the very first created being. This
view has the advantage of maintaining the dis-

tinct identities of Christ and God the Creator; they are not simply different modes of the same being, but one is created by the other. Christ is spoken of in scripture as "the first-born of all creation", and is, after all, referred to as the "only begotten Son" of God and as the "second Adam". In addition, this position provides a consitent backdrop against which to understand the possible conflict of wills implied by Christ's statement, "Not my will but Thine". On the debit side, however, this view raises the question of how or in what sense Christ himself can be thought of divine, if he is a created being. Moreover, Christ's claim to be "One with the Father" would seem to exclude his having been created.

Just to the right of center on the continuum is the position which maintains that Christ and the Creator, along with the Holy Spirit, are separate beings who have always <u>existed</u> <u>independently</u> of one another and who <u>together make up</u> the Godhead. The idea here seems to be a kind of "committee" view of the Godhead, each of the members of which is divine in its own right. In the creation story God says "Let <u>us</u> make human beings in <u>our</u> own image" and John says "In the <u>beginning</u> <u>was</u> the Word, and the Word was <u>with</u> God, and the Word was God". On the other hand, it can be argued that this view is essentially a "Tri-theism" and thus contravenes the monotheistic character of Judeo-Christian theology. What, after all, is the point of calling Christ the "Son" of God if he is co-eternal and independent with God the Creator?

Finally, just to the left of center, stands the position which develops the notion that Christ, while being of the same "substance" or nature as the Creator (and thus not created), is nevertheless an independent being by virtue of having a distinct volitional center, or personhood. The

28

focus of this view is the idea of emanation or flowing; as light flows from the sun while being both the same as and yet distinct from the sun, so Christ emanates from the Creator, equally divine but nonetheless distinct. The strength of this interpretation lies in its ability to avoid most of the difficulties confronting each of the other views. Its weakness is at the same place, namely in its eclecticism. For it may be merely an incoherent collection of incompatible notions. Which points up the viability of the insight that frequently Christian orthodoxy primarily consists in the assertion of paradox or mystery and in the negation of any and all views which seek to resolve such mystery into a straight-forward doctrine.

Along side of this overall issue of Christ's relation to the Creator stands the question of how his divinity and humanity are related. Here again there is a variety of views which can be placed along a continuum. At the extremes are those positions which assert either that Christ was God disguised as man (the more "conservative" view) or that Christ was a man who actualized the divine potential residing in every person (the more "liberal" view). Neither of these views has ever been in the mainstream of Christian theology, but they both keep reappearing.

The former conservative perspective arises out of a desire to preserve the divinity of Christ and out of a concern not to denigrate the concept of divinity by mixing it with lowly humanity. These purposes are accomplished by maintaining that Christ only "appeared" to become a man while in no way giving up his divinity and/or its prerogatives. Early on in Christian history this view, termed "docetism", was designeated as heresy, but it continues to appear in the theological marketplace. Its most recent expression can be found in certain circles of popular Evangelicalism. Not only is such a view difficult to jibe with particular passages of scripture, which specifically state that "the Word became flesh", etc., but it is out of keeping with the very idea of Incarnation and renders ineffective the whole notion of atonement as presented in scripture.

The latter liberal interpretation only became a major theme in Christian theology in modern times, especially at the turn of the century. The seeds of the Enlightenment and Renaissance joined together with the evolutionary motif of the 19th century to produce an over-abundance of confidence in the capabilities and Utopian future of humankind. Thus the understanding of Christ as the person who showed us how fully to actualize the divine principle in all creation came to make a great deal of sense to a large number of people. In addition to seeming a little naive in light of the conflicts and troubles of the 20th century, this view is quite difficult to square with the main historical and biblical themes of the Christian community. Christ's understanding of human nature and destiny hardly seems so optimistic, and his own nature seems much more complex and mysterious than this view allows.

Closer to the center of the continuum, and to the main stream of Christian thought, stand two other important positions. One of these maintains an inner/outer dualism between Christ's divinity and humanity. The idea here is that in his spiritual nature Christ was divine and possessed divine consciousness, while in his physical nature he was human, subject to human limitations, etc. This is perhaps the way most Christians think of Christ. It has the advantage of affirming both his divinity and his humanity without shortchanging either. It has the disadvantages, however, of leaving unexplained how the two natures are coordinated and of implying that somehow they are at odds with each other. The Gospels do not present Christ as having a higher and a lower nature, much less as in conflict with himself in any way.

The other more centrally located interpretation insists upon viewing Christ holistically, as an integrated person having but one nature. The stress here is upon the blending of the divine and human in such a way as to create an entirely new and unique personage. According to this view there was no conflict within Christ; the various dimensions of his being fully integrated with one another. Perhaps the analogy of blending of two human personages into one when a man and woman cause the birth to a child helps to illucidate this view. In some mysterious way the two become one without there being any way to say which part is which. Some take this holistic view as an escape from the responsibility of theological explanation, as a retreat into the realm of mystery in order to avoid the charge of the whole idea of incarnation being self-contradictory.

Finally, there is the issue of how the nature of Christ is to be understood in relation to revelation, from the point of view of those who claim to discern his divinity in his humanity. Once again it is helpful to compare the main theories along a continuum from right to left. The former extreme is represented by those who think of Christ's revelation of his divinity as done for the benefit of God the creator and the specifically chosen, the elect. Those theologians who stress God's sovereignty often take this view, arguing that in Christ God's revelation of divine loving nature is an end in itself, simply a witness of an already established truth. In essence then, according to this interpretation, Christ's incarnation and atonement constituted a private drama performed on God's behalf and that of those elected to receive salvation. Thus once again we see the humanity of Christ down-played and his divinity over-played.

At the opposite extreme is the interpretation which views the notion of Christ's divinity as simply a way of stressing his role as an example and inspiration for the rest of humanity. We are said to see in him all the great insights and aspirations of humankind, focused as never before. Here the notion of his divinity is down-played and his humanity is played up. This view will be recognized as a corollary of the liberal view of Christ discussed a bit earlier on. Neither of these two extreme interpretations has been dominant in Christian theology, primarily because they seem out of line with the central thrust of the scripture with respect to the complexity and importance of the notion of incarnation.

Traditionally most Christian theologians have maintained that Christ's divine nature is discerned or revealed on the basis of his activity amongst humans, by means of an inferential process. His miracles and teachings, it is claimed, serve as proof or evidence of his divinity to all who are open to the truth. Thus the facts of Christ's human life, as chronicled by the Gospel writers are said to provide the key to grasping his divinity. The words of John near the close of his Gospil are taken to summarize the relation between Christ's two natures: "These signs are written that you may believe that Jesus is the Christ, the Son of God, and that believing you may have life in his name: (John 20:31). This view has been termed the "Jesus of History" view.

Along side this more traditional interpretation, but slightly to the left, stands the position which emphasizes the "Christ of Faith" interpretation of Christ's nature. This view maintains that it is not the facts of Jesus' human activity which are important in discerning and appropriating his divinity, but the inward faith and self-understanding which result from a personal encounter with the Christian message. This is sometimes known as the "existentialist" posture in theology, and it has been forcefully focused in the work of Rudolph Bultmann and his notion of "demythologizing".

The stress here is on the subjective faith of the individual and not upon historical knowledge about Jesus. Christ's divinity, if it is to be so called, is discerned solely by the eye of faith and not from facts or by reason.

These latter two positions, while less extreme than the first two mentioned and while seemingly more sensitive to the biblical concept of Incarnation, are not without difficulties of their own. Both tend to leave unexamined, the nature of the connection between the Jesus of History and the Christ of Faith. One view stresses facts but is naive about how they lead to spiritual discernment, while the other view emphasizes faith but tends to compartmentalize it in relation to other dimensions of experience. The radical character of the Incarnation goes unexplored in either case. I shall try to indicate in Part Two how such an exploration might be begun. This seems to me to be the natural and essential place to begin a fresh and organic approach to theological inquiry.

Chapter Five

The Nature of Atonement

The nature of Christ's redemptive work lies at the very heart of Christian theology. The scripture employs a rather wide variety of metaphors in speaking of the atonement--the act whereby God and humanity are brought into "at-one-ment". The main theological points of view on the atonement tend to cluster around a half-dozen of these metaphors, and our discussion of the points of view will consist of a survey of the dominant metaphors. While the emphases amongst these interpretations of redemption vary considerably, none of them are necessarily mutually exclusive of the others.

Two of the more frequent approaches to the atonement can be said to emphasize its "objective" character. One of these has been termed the Ransom Theory, for it centers on the passages which speak of Christ being "a ransom for many". This view was more popular during the early centuries of Christian history than it has been recently. It was generally said that Satan had taken humans captive and God paid a ransom through the death of Christ in order to free us from the control of Satan. Many of the criticisms of this view focus on the question of how God could have been in a position to have to meet conditions set by Satan in order to accomplish the redemptive purpose. Pushed far enough back, this question leads directly to the traditional "problem of evil" and to dualistic theories of divinity.

The other objectivist interpretation is usually referred to as the "penal satisfaction" view of the atonement. This view keys off of those scripture passages which depict Christ as a "propitiation" or "sacrifice" offered by God on behalf of humankind in order to satisfy the just demands of divine holiness. Since God is holy and humans are sinners, there is said to exist a great gulf between the two. Out of holy love God sent Christ to "pay the price" for our sinfulness by his own death, thereby fulfilling both the justice and love of God. The picture here is of a judge who pardons the offender, not by dismissing the case but by providing the necessary retribution. In this way Christ is said to be our "substitute" in that he took the punishment--death--which was rightfully ours. This interpretation became important during the Middle Ages, played a significant role in the Reformation, and remains the dominant view in conservative theological circles today.

Although it cannot be denied that there are passages in scripture which support this interpretation, it is also true that an exclusive reliance on it obscures other important dimensions of the atonement. More specifically, in addition to having a tendency to portray God as something of a schizophrenic legalist who is primarily interested in keeping cosmic books balanced, this view has little or nothing to say about the purpose and effects of redemption vis à vis human beings. It would seem, after all, that the primary purpose of redemption would be a qualitative change in the character of those redeemed, not just an official or forensic change in their status. Finally, it can be objected that this view over-emphasizes the death of Christ almost to the exclusion of the value of his life. It would almost seem that according to this position Jesus could have been killed as an infant and still have effected the atonement.

It is questions such as the above which have given rise to what may be termed the "subjective" interpretations of Christ's redemptive work. One of these positions has been called the "Moral

36

Influence" theory because it stresses the role of Christ as an example and inspiration for all humankind. Thus the atonement is seen from this point of view as God's effort to influence the moral character of persons by means of the life and death of Christ. Here the emphasis is on the quality of Christ's life--and the continuity of his death with his life--as the agent of redemption. The crucifixion only takes on significance in light of the ethical teachings and activities of Christ's life. Through Christ God "reconciled the world unto Himself", namely by showing the way toward a more Godly life.

A major difficulty with this interpretation is that it fails to account for the uniqueness of Christ's life and work. That is to say, if all his redemptive work consisted of was moral example and inspiration, he is of no greater significance than a long list of partriarchs, prophets, and apostles. To come at it from another angle, it would seem that the real force of Christ's moral influence must be based in some cosmic reality which transcends the merely human realm in order to have significance and potency. In a word, this view seems to leave out the depth and richness entailed in the notion of atonement.

A slightly different "subjective" interpretation is that offered by what are called "Holiness" theologies. This approach focuses on the passages which emphasize the "making whole" motif of salvation. Those who are "believers in Christ" no longer live according to the flesh, but are led by and filled with the Holy Spirit, and they produce the fruits thereof. For this reason they are called "Saints", "God's people", and are said to comprise "the Bride" and "the Body" of Christ. In short this position maintains that the atoning work of Christ includes the making whole, or sanctification, of those who participate in it. The atonement is not simply for God's benefit, but is primarily aimed at redeeming, and thus changing the character of, those persons who accept it.

Criticims of the above position are generally aimed at its failure to do justice to the deep-rooted nature of sin and the growth-process character of redemption. It is argued that there is a distinction between justification and sanctification in Christian theology. The former is a state and was accomplished once and for all in Christ's death, while the latter is a process and will continue until God established the kingdom. We must continually be appropriating our new life in Christ, since our being made whole does not happen all at once. In a sense no one knows better how ambiguous and deceitful the human heart is than the Christian. As someone once put it, the only real difference between non-Christians and Christians is that the latter are confessing sinners.

Over against these objectivist and subject-ivist theories stand those which center more on the "deliverance" metaphors found in scripture. Rather than focusing on the results of the atone-ment in relation either to God or humankind, this approach seeks to emphasize the redeeming activity of Christ. In this way the effects of the atone-ment are said to be seen in their proper light. Much of the impetus for this approach comes from interpreting the passages which speak of Christ dying "for" us as meaning "on our behalf" rather than "instead of" us. In other words, the empha-sis is not on a substitutionary view of the atone-ment, but on its reconciling character as focused in Christ's activity of living and dying.

One posture within this general approach is that which stresses the victory of Christ over the powers of evil. It can be termed the conquest interpretation of the atonement. Humankind is viewed as having been held captive by the forces of sin and death. Christ then is said to attack these powers with love and forgiveness, and to thereby deliver humankind from them. The atonement is thus seen as the victory of Christ, by means of his sacrificial love, over the powers of evil. Humans are reconciled to God in the sense of being reunited with God, and are now free to grow into fullness of life.

Another posture within the general "deliverance" approach is what might be termed the "absorption" posture. The emphasis here is upon the notion that Christ took our sins upon himself in order to free us from their domination. Christ is said to have borne our sins, not in the sense of bearing the punishment for them, but in the sense of taking them into his person, of absorbing them. He delivers us from evil, not so much by conquering it, nor by removing us from its influence, but by continually drawing it into himself. Through his own active and unending love Christ defuses and dissipates sin and suffering. Thus, according to this interpretation, the Christian answer to the infamous "problem of evil" is to acknowledge the reality of evil and to affirm Christ's realistic efforts to neutralize it through sacrificial love. Moreover, he enlists the help of those who seek to follow him in this continuing and crucial task.

While not wishing to deny any of the above insights, proponents of the objectivist theories of the atonement would argue that such deliverance theories fail to do justice to those passages wherein Christ's work is described as being a "propitiation" to God on humankind's behalf, as a payment for sin. In like manner, subjectivists would argue that deliverance oriented theories do not provide sufficiently for character change in believers. To be freed from the domination of evil must include more than simply providing for its continual absorption or conquest. Something must be done to irradicate evil from human life if redemption is to be effective.

It may well be that it is impossible to synthesize all these views into one coherent and comprehensive doctrinal statement. Yet each line of interpretation brings with it something unique, and thus none can be dispensed with. As long as the different perspectives do not logically exclude one another--and it does not seem all of them do--then no harm is done by maintaining a place for each within Christian theology. In fact, such a rich assortment of ways of thinking about the atonement is entirely in keeping with the richness and profoundity of the notion itself. In Chapter Nine I shall seek to refocus this issue from another angle.

Chapter Six

The Nature of Christian Responsibility

The primary concern of Christian Ethics is how to understand the meaning of Jesus' command that we love our neighbor (including our enemies) "as ourselves". Although the issues of the nature of self-love and the viability of a command to love are important in and of themselves, they are perhaps best treated in relation to a broader question, namely the application of the notion of love to social and political responsibility. It is one thing to speak of love in individual, personal relations and quite another to seek its implementation in public policy. In point of fact, it is not clear to what extent Jesus meant his ethical teaching, as focussed in the "Sermon on the Mount", to apply to the social dimension of existence.

There are those who maintain that the ideal of love is both realizable and practical in all dimensions of Christian living, including the social. In modern times both the pacifist tradition and the "social gospel" of liberalism have espoused this interpretation, while recently they have been joined by "liberation theologians" of all stripes. The central thrust of this approach is to stress the straight-forward, unqualified character of Jesus' command to love and to be perfect in the "Sermon on the Mount". He did not preface his teaching with circumstantial parameters about when they do apply and when they do not. He simply commanded that we love; and unrelentingly spelled-out the implications of this radical posture vis à vis our motivations as well as our actions.

It is argued that anything less than this straight-forward interpretation both misses the essence of the Christian ethic and runs counter to the history of Christian experience. There is nothing new nor especially powerful about a concept of love which accommodates itself to the extenuating circumstances of human existence apart from Christ. The whole point of the Christian "way" is that it calls for a radical departure from ordinary and traditional concepts of what constitutes "the good life". Jesus himself never sought to qualify his fundamental teaching in his own life, but rather he embodied the love ethic in every detail right up to, and especially in, his death. Moreover, it has always been the case that when the Christian community committed itself without reservation to the ideal of love it grew in both quantity and quality. The example of the early Christian centuries makes this abundantly clear; persecutions produced purity and growth.

According to this point of view, the results of the straight-forward application of Jesus' ethic of love to every aspect of life will be a world of peace and goodwill. The dream of the Old Testament phophets of the coming Kingdom of God and Jesus' vision of the Kingdom of Heaven will come together and a New Age will be ushered in. Love will replace the need for justice, since war, crime, and all other inhumanities to man will be left behind. The urgency of the Christian ethic derives from the need for us to co-operate with God in concrete expression of love so as to hasten and actualize God's kingdom. Thus the ideal of love is thought to be both realizable and practical vis à vis transforming our present world into the new Heaven and the new Earth.

The major line of criticism which is usually leveled at the above interpretation of the Christian concept of love is that it is quite unrealistic.

Put bluntly, the objection is that to live a life of complete love is impossible. Even if it is possible for a few, so-called "Saints", it is simply beyond the experience of the rank and file of Christians. To set such an ideal before believers is to court failure, despair, and spiritual frustration. Moreover, since the world is full of folk who do (if not seek) evil, to take up a posture of pure love would necessitate withdrawing from the world. This would inevitably lead to there being more evil in the world, since sometimes the only way to control evil is by force or violence.

At the opposite extreme, then, are those who interpret the "Sermon on the Mount" and the command of absolute love as an unrelizable and impractical ideal. There are two distinct lines of reasoning within this general interpretation. The first has been most forcefully expressed in recent times by what is called "Neo-orthodox theology." The emphasis here is on an individualistic understanding of the Christian gospel in general and of its ethical implications in particular. It is maintained that Christ's commandments are meant strictly for individual believers to apply in their personal lives, they have nothing to say about how society ought or ought not be structured. To attempt to organize our national and international life around absolute love is to confuse the revelation of God's character with practical policy. We must maintain a clear line of separation between what theologians Karl Barth and Reinhold Niebuhr called, respectively, "the Word of God and the word of man, on the one hand, and "the children of light and the children of darkness" on the other.

The second line of reasoning within this overall posture is that taken by certain Fundamentalists known as "dispensationalists". Without going into all the ins-and-outs of this general approach, it will be sufficient to point out that it maintains that during different periods of history God has dealt with humankind according to different principles or dispensations. The "Sermon on the Mount" was given at the beginning of the Church Period of history (a sort of parenthesis between the first and second coming of Christ) in order to explain the character of God's kingdom which will be set up after Christ's second coming. Thus the commandment of absolute love applies only to the period or dispensation of the kingdom, Christ's thousand year reign on earth which lies entirely in the future. It is, therefore, unrealizable and impractical in the present age.

The purpose of Christ's commandments, according to this interpretation, is not only to reveal the character of the coming kingdom, but to point up the limitations of human goodness apart from the full reign of Christ in his kingdom. Just as the law served to establish the need for the Gospel, so "the Sermon on the Mount" establishes the need for the kingdom. All of this is not to imply, however, that Christians can be totally oblivious to the fruits of the spirit, chief among which is love. It is only to insist that such fruits must inevitably be sought in individual lives and must not be thought of as the standard by which all humans are to be judged in this time in history.

A common line of criticism of this general interpretation is that it is an obscurantist, isolationist rationalization of the clear teachings of Christ. Not only does Jesus nowhere preface his teachings on love with comments relegating them to some future kingdom, but to argue that the commandment of absolute love is irrelevant to the Christian's responsibility in the world in which he or she lives is to undercut the whole notion of Christian influence. After all, believers are said to be the salt of the earth. The interpretation under consideration has the effect of cutting the moral nerve of Christian faith, rendering it a dead faith without works. In like fashion, to limit Christian love to "personal ethics" (a strange phrase at best) is to dichotomize the believer's life into two opposing spheres and may possibly lead to increased evil in the world. Such a dichotomy is out of line with the main thrust of the Incarnation, namely that the Word _became_ flesh.

In between these two rather extreme interpretations stands what has been called the "Biblical Realist" position, affirming both the unrealizable and the practical character of the ideal of love. The heart of this stance is the denial that unrealizability entails impracticality. The claim here is that the unrealizable ideal of absolute love fulfills a two-fold function for the Christian believer in both her or her personal and social responsibilities. Its negative function is to serve as a constant and unaltering reminder of our frailty, of our need of forgiveness and grace. At the end of the day when we know that we have not loved perfectly and this knowledge is the ground of our reaffirmation of our co-operative dependency on God. The negative function of the ideal is to provide us with a contrite heart.

The positive function of the unrealizable ideal of absolute love is to serve as a goal toward which to strive. Even though we know we shall never attain a given goal, that does not mean that it is useless to aim at it. For in and by striving for the unattainable we can, in fact, get closer to it; we can in fact grow more loving by seeking to fulfill the commandment of absolute love. Amongst the choices and situations with which we are faced, some more nearly approximate the ideal than others; our responsibility is to work at actualizing those which do. Sometimes, of course, our choices will be between alternatives neither of which embodies much, if any, love. Even in these cases, however, one alternative will be less evil than the other, and the ideal of love enables us to choose between the two.

Those who advocate this interpretation of Christian ethical responsibility argue that it is supported by both scripture and experience. Jesus never qualified his commandment of absolute love, and the New Testament gives every indication that forgiveness will always be necessary, even for believers. In addition, when we are truely being honest we will all admit that we live as if absolute love is both beyond us in principle and a vital part of our Christian growth. Thus it is unrealizable but practical as an ideal.

Perhaps the strongest criticism that can be brought against the above interpretation--aside from those which flow naturally from the positive expression of the competing views--is that at its best this approach leaves the Christian in great tension, striving to grow towards an ideal while knowing full well that it cannot be attained. Such tension not only may create deep sense of frustration, but it may also lead to a doctrine of growth in "salvation by works". After all, the Gospel is meant to liberate humans from the oppression of self-justificatory striving. At its worst, this interpretation might be said to exemplify a self-fulfilling prophecy. If one declares at the outset that an ideal is unrealizable it most likely will turn out to be so.

We shall return to this question of the basis and nature of Christian ethics in Part Two (Chapter Twelve), where I shall offer some concrete suggestions for a different, though not unrelated approach.

Chapter Seven

The Kingdom of God

Closely related to the question of Christian responsibility, as discussed in the previous chapter, is the question of the nature and timing of the Kingdom of God. This theme is usually given the name "Eschatology" in Christian theology, a name which signifies the doctrine of "last things" or of "the end times". Another way to approach the question is to ask when and in what way will God's activity in human history be culminated and fulfilled.

One point of view on such questions is that which traditionally has been given the name "post-millenarianism". This is the view that God's kingdom is present in history at this time. According to this position Christ's first coming into the world fulfilled the Old Testament promises of a Messiah who would re-establish the kingdom of David. Thus we are said to be in the kingdom period now. Christ's second coming will mark the culmination of this period. Between the two comings of Christ the kingdom is said to be growing, and when it reaches its full maturity Christ will return to earth. In other words, he will return after or as the kingdom is fully realized (thus the term "post-Millenarianism"; 'Millenium' means a thousand year period).

In addition to the Old Testament promises of a messiah and a kingdom, which Christ claimed to fulfill, Christ's teachings concerning the kingdom of God being "at hand" and "within you" provide the main lines of support for this point of view. Moreover, the kingdom is described as beginning as a grain of mustard seed and growing into full bloom, even as we see the spread of the

gospel and the development of the church throughout the ages. Finally, the descriptions of the
end times in the book of Revelation and in Paul's
letters to the Thessalonians have the second coming of Christ, the final judgment, and the beginning of the new heaven and new earth occuring in
uninterrupted sequence. If the kingdom is not
now present, there is no other time in which it
could take place.

A practical argument which is often used to
support this interpretation of the kingdom runs
like this. To place the kingdom of God entirely
in the future is to encourage Christians to be
inactive in or withdraw from the present world
situation. Such "quietism" is a luxury Christians
can ill afford in a world full of misery and evil.
To believe that the kingdom is present in history
is to be called to participate in its development.
After all, Paul says "we are co-laborers with God"
in bringing the kingdom to earth.

Those who criticize this interpretation usually do so for two reasons. First, it can be
argued that this position is too optimistic in
its understanding of Western civilization. While
the idea of human progress, and this the inevitable growth of the kingdom of God, was more popular and may have been more tenable during the
17th, 18th, and especially the 19th centuries,
it is difficult to espouse it today. Two World
Wars, an international depression, the threat of
"the Bomb", the energy and ecological crises--all
of these have called assumptions about the inev-
itability of progress into serious question.
Indeed, it might even be possible to argue that
current anthropological evidence indicates that
other cultures and other times may well have been,
in their own way, every bit as enlightened and
humane (or unenlightened and inhumane) as ours is.

Secondly, from a theological perspective it can be maintained that the position in question comes too close to equating Christianity and contemporary culture. Such an equation systematically eliminates any vantage point from which to evaluate one's particular culture negatively. To identity the kingdom of God with the "progress" of a given culture or civilization is to overplay the "created order" at the expense of neglecting the "fallen order". In Christian theology good and evil are dimensions of human nature which comprise the matrix of experience on both the individual and social levels. Another way to phrase this point is to remind ourselves that the judgmental perspective of the prophetic voice must always be allowed to speak if humans are to avoid taking themselves too seriously and the temptation to "play God". In an interpretation of the kingdom which too closely relates it to the present this prophetic perspective is precluded.

A significantly different interpretation is offered by those who take what is frequently called a "pre-Millenarian" position on the kingdom of God. According to this view, the kingdom is seen as strictly a futuristic reality, as something which will come to pass after human history. Those who take this position maintain that Christ's first coming introduced the period of the Church, a period we are still in, and that his second coming will take place just prior to (or will usher in) the Kingdom of God. Thus this view is termed "pre-Millenarianism"; Christ will come before his thousand year rule on earth, a period which will come between the present age of the church and the creation of the new heaven and the new earth.

Incidentally, there is considerable debate amongst pre-Millenarianists about whether Christ's second coming will take place before, mid-way through, or at the end of a brief (seven year?)

49

period known as "the tribulation", which they all agree will immediately precede the setting up of Christ's kingdom. This period of tribulation is said to be characterized by rampant evil and a great war (Armageddon) between the forces of good (Christ's army) and the forces of evil (Satan's army). This interpretation draws heavily on Jesus' and Paul's teachings, especially in the latter chapters of Matthew and the letters to the Thessalonians and to Timothy, about the great persecutions which will face Christians "in that day".

Pre-Millenarianism is a form of "Dispensationalism", which was introduced in the previous chapter. Thus its proponents draw upon the teachings and implications of Dispensationalism doctrine for support. God deals with humankind differently in different ages according to the divine plan or "economy"; and thus the periods of the church (now), the kingdom, and the intervening tribulation each has its own principles and limitations.

Perhaps the key piece of evidence employed to establish this interpretation is the initiation and continuation of the Zionistic nation in Jerusalem. Pre-Millenarians argue that both the Old Testament and Paul's teachings in Romans make it clear that the Jewish nation will play an important point in the final events of history. Moreover, they claim that the apocalyptic books of Daniel, Ezekiel, and Revelation teach that Christ will reign in Jerusalem for a thousand years, after Armageddon and before the creation of the new heaven and a new earth.

Supporters of this point of view frequently point out that our times, especially the last fifty or sixty years, are particularly well-described by the statement of Jesus and Paul about the "latter days" being characterized by "wars and rumors of wars", famine, pestilence, and increased bureaucracy. These characteristics are taken as direct evidence of the coming tribulation and second advent of Christ, prior to the establishment of his kingdom.

There are three main lines of attack used by those who would seek to discredit this interpretation of the Kingdom of God. The first is simply to indicate that it is a far too pessimistic point of view. The point here is that this interpretation almost completely ignores the "created order" of human existence because it overplays the "fallen order". After all, humans were made in God's image and this world is still God's in some sense. To place the kingdom entirely in the future is to cut the nerve of moral obligation for the Christian in today's world. If everything is doomed to get worse and worse until the end comes, why should we bother to overcome any evil here and now?

A second move is to point out that this position completely overlooks the concrete teachings of Christ when he said, during his first advent, that the Kingdom of God is "at hand" and "within you". In fact, Jesus actually said once that his disciples would not taste death until they see Christ come in all his glory. If this was meant to refer to the second coming, obvious problems arise. Moreover, much of Christ's own teaching was concerned with making significant changes in the here and now. Why would he have bothered if the kingdom is entirely in the future?

Thirdly, it has often been pointed out that this whole approach to theology is based on a faulty, "literalist" interpretation of scripture. The complaint here is that to treat the Bible as if it were some sort of "divine ougie board" from which one can squeeze out informational truths and predictions about the future is to do the scriptures a great injustice and cast dispersions upon God's way of revealing divine truth.

51

The Bible is a rich and complex book containing forms of literature, each of which must be interpreted according to principles suitable to its nature. Nowhere is this point more flagrantly violated than in the pre-Millenarian manipulation of self-acknowledged apocalyptic literature, such as <u>Daniel</u>, <u>Ezekiel</u>, and <u>Revelation</u>. To use these books as allegories and exercises in numerology is to ignore their historical and political significance for their own time--and to obviate their symbolic (not <u>allegorical</u>) value for those in other times.

Lastly, a brief account of a more recent and highly influential interpretation, namely that of Christian Existentialist Theology, is in order before bringing Part One to a close. Following the lead of Rudolph Bultmann many contemporary theologians have maintained what is called "<u>Realized Eschatology</u>". The central thrust here is aimed at disengaging (demythologizing) the Christian message from the mythological "packaging" it received at the hands of First and Second century biblical writers. Such a move carries especially powerful implications for interpretations of the notion of the Kingdom.

The central concern of existentialist exegesis is to render the scriptural teachings relevant to modern humankind. Thus all those aspects of biblical passages which reflect the world-view of the First century are to be set aside as so much "husk" in order to enable the "kernel" of the Gospel to be properly appreciated. The heart of the Christian message pertains to the quality and stance of one's life, not to what one happens to believe about the make-up of the cosmos, futuristic events, etc. Authentic living is what the Christian Gospel is about, not intellectual beliefs about this world or the next.

Thus, according to this interpretation, both post- and pre- Millenarianism are entirely beside the point. Both take the biblical talk about the kingdom literally, rather than seeing it simply as the mythological trappings of Jewish apocalyticism in which the Gospel was wrapped. The whole notion of the kingdom was a hold-over from Jewish historical experience (David and the captivities) and needs to be discarded now that the cosmology of a three-storied universe (heaven, earth, hell) has been discredited by modern science. Today we need to see the kingdom as simply a spiritual symbol of a certain quality of life which should characterize Christian people.

Three problems can be raised for this interpretation. One is the problem of the role of science. There is reason to believe that Existentialist theologians have granted too much authority to the modern, scientific world-view, failing to see that it, too, is a mythological child of its time. In other words, although accommodation is necessary to communication, it would appear that the biblical passages are receiving the short end of the stick in this exchange. Another closely related problem is that of the relation between truth and myth. These thinkers seem to assume that one can simply extract truth out of a mythological setting, like a kernel out of a husk. But it is possible, and indeed more likely, that the relation between truth and the context within which it arises is more akin to that of an onion and its layers. As one peels away the layers one also peels away the onion.

Thirdly, the Existentialist interpretation assumes a neat and complete dichotomy between one's intellectual beliefs and one's authenticity in life. While it may not be possible or desirable to equate the two, it hardly seems advisable to separate them absolutely. Such a procedure creates a kind of schizophrenia all too common in our culture.

Theological beliefs, and in particular, views about the nature of the kingdom, are relevant to the business of living authentically, in the same way that knowledge and well grounded beliefs about another person are relevant (though admittedly not sufficient) to a meaningful relationship with that person. The two are not mutually exclusive--and neither are the notions of a present kingdom and a future one. But more of that at the close of Part Two.

This concludes our brief survey of the main themes of traditional Christian theology from a systematic perspective. Hopefully the main issues, postures, and problems have been sufficiently introduced and clarified to enable us to move ahead to a more organic exploration of these themes, based in a Christological point of departure.

Part Two

An

Organic Exploration

Chapter Eight

Christ at the Center:

The Incarnation

At I mentioned in the Introduction, in the second half of this book I shall seek to explore the main themes of Christian theology by means of an organic model. By this I mean a model which places Christ's life and work at the center (at the heart) and then attempts to relate each of the other themes to that center in the way spokes connect the hub with the rim of a wheel, or as the various members of a human body integrate with one another. In other words, in each case the particular doctrine in question needs to be understood in terms of the Incarnation and Atonement of Christ and not vice versa. This alternative approach invariably changes the way we think and speak about some of the main Christian themes introduced in Part One.

The central task of all theological thinking about the Incarnation is to speak meaningfully and responsibly about the phrase "God was in Christ reconciling the world unto Himself". More specifically, the task is to unpack the little word 'in' so as to do justice to the demands of meaning while at the same time acknowledging the inevitable mystery involved in this key phrase. Perhaps the most important thing to keep in mind is that any view which claims to explain the Incarnation fully is certainly going to be inadequate.

The point of focus of all theories of the Incarnation is the claim that Jesus Christ was (and is) both divine and human. The crucial question is how these two natures could be combined in one personage. Throughout the history of the Christian church all those interpretations which have emphasized the priority of one of these natures to the other have been deemed inadequate and misleading. The pendulum tends to swing from one extreme to the other from one age to the next; and one important rule of thumb might simply be to avoid extremes while seeking to say something significant and helpful.

In the following exploration I shall present four themes that seem to me to be central to the Christian notion of Incarnation, especially as it is presented in the Gospel accounts. I shall seek to avoid the difficulties attendent to the various views discussed in Chapter Four, while establishing a meaningful axis around which to locate the other theological doctrines with which we shall be dealing. The four themes that I shall present may seem obvious or rather radical, depending on one's point of view, but I submit that they are pivotal in the development of a truely Christian theology.

To begin with, whatever else we may wish to say about the way in which God was in Jesus Christ, it seems necessary to insist that it took place in a <u>holistic</u> manner. That is to say, there was nothing fragmented or divided about the person of Jesus, no divine side and no human side, as would be the case with a dualistic interpretation. In a word, the person of Jesus Christ <u>integrated</u> the divine and human natures into one center of volition and consciousness. The Gospels never present Jesus as sometimes acting as a god and sometimes as a human, or as some sort of schizophrenic, with conflicting personalities. Rather, he is presented as an integrated, focused being who has his own self and his own will, but one who was continuously committing himself to the will of God.

Christ's struggle in the Garden of Gethsemane makes it clear, as perhaps no other passage does,

that although he ultimately chose to follow the
way of the cross, God's will for him, Christ could
have chosen not to follow this course of action.
He was his own, integrated person. Even though we
cannot say what the full meaning or consequence of
such a choice would have been, to deny that it was
a real possibility is to turn the Gethsemane
struggle into a cosmic charade. Moreover, the Gospel accounts of this struggle say nothing about Jesus having a divine will and a human. When he said
"not my will but thine", he was exercising his own
will in commitment to God, not denying some weaker,
human will.

A second important theme in the Christian
notion of Incarnation is that it was contextual.
By this term I mean to call attention to the fact
that the biblical understanding of God's activity
in Jesus Christ necessitates actual divine involvement in the human world, our world. God was not in
Christ in the way Superman was in Clark Kent, (disguised as "the mild-mannered reporter from the
Daily Planet") or in the way certain deities of
other religions occasionally appear in human form,
only shortly to dematerialize again. The Christian
claim is that in Jesus Christ God entered into the
concrete context of our world, into space and time
in general and at a specific place and period of
history in particular.

God's entrance into the time dimension distinguishes the Christian faith from other religions. For, it focuses and sanctifies the temporal
world in a way largely absent from other religious
traditions. Whereas some faiths stress the priority of a single phase of time (past, present, or
future) and others see time as cyclical, Christianity
follows the Hebrew tradition in emphasizing the
importance of history. Time is linear, it is going
somewhere, and what happens in time is taken as
extremely significant. In fact, the Judeo-Christian
tradition the very definition of divine revelation

itself involves the "mighty acts of God" in human history. Place, too, is taken as religiously significant in the Judeo-Christian tradition, but not as strongly as in many other faiths. In fact, whereas there are holy places in Judaism, the Christian faith tends to turn the notion of "holy space" from a physical reality toward a spiritual one in the concept of the kingdom of God. But more of this in Chapter Fourteen.

The concrete contextuality of the Incarnation renders time, place, and people religiously significant. What people, especially Christ, did and said, where they went and when, all are of importance in coming to an understanding of revelation and faith. They are not strictly important in and of themselves, but neither are they unimportant, as with many other religious traditions. Rather, they are significant as mediators of divine reality. The when and wheres, the hows and whats, the whos and whys of Christ's life are the intersections at which or the transparencies through which we encounter God.

Thirdly, God's entrance into our world in the Incarnation was embodied in character. Actually, this is just another way of stressing the root meaning of the term 'Incarnation' -- God in the flesh. Here again we see the concrete nature of the Christian notion of revelation. Christian faith does not focus on a collection of abstract teachings nor on private spiritual experiences of God or truth, etc. It focuses, rather, on a life lived by a specific person in a specific time and place -- and in a body. What Jesus did, where and when, how and to whom, and why are of supreme importance. In short, that God was in Christ in an embodied form pinpoints the fact that the human form of life, involving bodies and social interaction, is both the matrix and the crucible for revelation and faith.

We are accustomed in Christian circles to think of the body, human flesh, as evil. We have inherited this way of thinking from Greek philosophy by way of medieval theologians such as Augustine and Aquinas. That it is not a biblical way to think should be evident from the simple fact that the heart of the Christian Gospel is the claim that in Christ God "became flesh and dwelt among us." There is nothing inherently evil about the physical dimension of our existence, as both the Creation and the Incarnation show. This dimension, like any other, is susceptible to perversion and distortion, but it need not express itself in this way, as the person of Christ clearly demonstrates. Moreover, Paul speaks of the church as the "body of Christ", of presenting our bodies as "living sacrifices" to God, and of our eventual bodily resurrection. In fact, Jesus Christ himself had (and would seem to still have) a resurrected body.

One corollary of the embodied character of God's presence in Christ is that of limitation. The Gospels do not present Jesus as having a divine, all-knowing mind, as being able to transcend human limitations at will. He readily admits that there are things he does not know (when he shall return to earth, e.g.), he experiences deep frustration over the unbelief of the Jewish people, he weeps, he hungers and thirsts, gets tired, etc. Most important, Jesus is presented as vulnerable, as open to risk, and as experiencing death. He did not merely survive death, he died (literally) and was raised again.

Finally, a fourth theme in the Christian understanding of the Incarnation is that of mediation. Two New Testament passages speak especially helpfully about this aspect of the Incarnation. In the first chapter of John's gospel we are told that "the Word", the same force through whom the world was created, "became flesh and dwelt among us." Much hangs on the choice of imagery--the pre-existent and creative Christ is said to be "the Word" or rationale of God. There is a direct parallel between this passage and the first chapter of Genesis wherein God creates the world through speech. The root metaphor of the Hebrew mode of thought is that of speech ("Hear O Israel, the Lord your god is One"), as opposed to the Greek reliance on vision. Ancient peoples very often reflect a deep respect for the creative, orphic power of language. Moreover, calling Christ "the Word" brings to the fore that God is communicating through a medium, not directly. All language stands in need of interpretation and is subject to misunderstanding.

This passage in John also says that the Word became flesh. All words must take a concrete form, must enter into the real world, if they are to bear meaning. Thus all utterances both reveal and veil in the sense that the more specific they become about one subject the less they can say about other subjects. In like manner, Christ's Incarnation, in order to bear significance, had to take on a specific shape in a specific time and place (Palestine, during the Roman occupation, in the Aramaic and Greek languages, etc.). This specificity necessarily colors the character of what is said, but not in such a way that we can disengage the one from the other. Furthermore, although misunderstanding is possible it is not necessary.

Jesus Christ was a concrete, fully human person yet he mediated or communicated more than simple humanity, he focused the divine. For the passage goes to say, "We beheld his glory, glory as of the only begotten of the Father, full of grace and truth." Even though the Incarnation necessarily veils much of God's personhood and character because of the limitations of concrete, historical expression, it reveals God adequately to those who are seeking spiritual truth with an open and sincere heart and mind. Nevertheless, it is important to stress that this revelation is <u>mediated</u> <u>in</u> <u>and</u> <u>through</u> the particulars of Jesus life and death, it is not directly observable nor is it a conclusion to be inferred from those particulars as from empirical data. The meaning of a specific linguistic expression does not lie on the "surface" of the words used, nor "behind" them to be deduced from them, but is rather discerned through an awareness of the use to which the expression is put within a concrete context. In like manner, the meaning of God's Incarnate Word in Jesus Christ does not lie on the surface of, nor does it "lurk" mysteriously behind, the particulars of that Incarnation, but it is discerned as mediated <u>in</u> <u>and</u> <u>through</u> those particulars.

Perhaps this notion of mediation can be clarified by examples taken from aesthetic experience. The harmony of a painting or a piece of music does not and cannot exist apart from the particulars, such as shapes, colors, tones, pitch, and relationships amongst them, of which it is comprised. Nonetheless, harmony cannot be pointed to directly, as can these particulars, nor can it be deduced or strictly inferred from them. Rather, harmony is best said to be experienced <u>in</u> <u>and</u> <u>through</u> these particulars and the concrete configuration which they take in the work of art in question. So it is with the meaning of the Incarnation, of the Word becoming flesh.

The second chapter of <u>Philippians</u> speaks of Christ as taking "the form of a servant, being born in the likeness of men." This passage amplifies the themes of the first chapter of <u>John</u>. Not only does it state that Christ "emptied himself" of, or set aside his divine perogatives in order to participate in the Incarnation, but it stresses that he took the most humble human form, that of a servant. Perhaps one would expect the Incarnate

63

Word to take the form of a king, but instead his revelation was veiled in the sense that Jesus was essentially a "nobody" from a back-water town in an obscure and internationally unimportant country. Nothing in Jesus' life, death, or resurrection establishes his divinity beyond a shadow of a doubt. Even his post-resurrection appearances were reserved for those who had made a commitment to him. In fact, the whole tenor and the final outcome of Christ's ministry were, by all political and religious standards, hardly what we would call "successful".

This emphasis on the servant character and tragic ending of Jesus' life underlines the mediated nature of Incarnational revelation. For, if one simply reads these events on the surface one will surely fail to discern their spiritual meaning. Rather, one must "read between the lines," much the way we do when grasping the significance of an ironic utterance. In a sense, the Incarnation is essentially an ironic event--one which means just the opposite of what it seems to say. This meaning is mediated more by the way the Incarnation was accomplished--its quality and tone-- than by what actually transpired. The divine and human were united an a unique, fresh phenomenon, the God-human Jesus Christ. The Incarnation is a mystery which must not be explained away by reducing one dimension of its meaning to another.

Perhaps an analogy will cast some light on-- but in no way "explain"-- this mystery. Consider the way in which the being and personality of both the mother and father of a baby are united into one, yet distinct person when the baby is conceived. The mystery of conception is nonetheless real for not being factually and exhaustively explainable. In the final analysis the scientist must simply say "This is what happens when the two sets of chromosomes combine; why it happens in precisely this way and not some other--or not at all!--is not a scientific question." As the baby grows into a child and then into an adult,

the various traits of each parent are inextricably blended with those of the other so as to make
the questions about which part or how much of the
child is from the mother and/or father basically
irrelevant. Yet we do not deny either that the
child is a mixture of both or that he or she is
nonetheless a unique person as well.

To borrow a phrase from Paul, "Now we see
through a glass, darkly." In the Incarnation we
discern the divine dimensions in and through the
human dimension. Thus we do see God sufficiently
for faith to have a solid experiential basis, but
we still see incompletely, "darkly", as well.
Incarnational revelation is mediated revelation.

Chapter Nine

Christ for Us: The Atonement

     The various interpretations of Christ's rec-
onciling work generally draw upon one or two of
the many different metaphors used in the New Testament to express the significance of the claim
that "God was in Christ reconciling the world
unto Himself." The chief difficulty in working
out a balanced and thorough view of the Atonement
lies in avoiding an over-emphasis on any one metaphor while attempting to do at least minimal justice to the main ones. It is important to bear
in mind both that the main metaphors are not mutually exclusive and that when dealing with a
complex and rich dimension of experience varied
metaphors are necessary to allow such richness
and complexity to reveal itself.

     To my way of thinking it is difficult, if
not impossible, to come to an adequate understanding of God's reconciling work in Christ without
first getting clear about the need for such reconciliation. In traditional theological parlance
this is called establishing the nature of sin.
Frequently Christian thinkers, even those as un-
alike as Billy Graham and Reinhold Niebuhr, will
explain sin, or our estrangement from God and
others, in terms of a single, isolatable behav-
ioral act of disobedience and/or pride. Whether
one interprets the story of the origin of sin,
found in Genesis (Chapter Three) as an historical
narrative ("literally") or as a cosmic myth
("symbolically"), the basic cause of our estrangement is said to be our desire (or Adam and Eve's
desire) to take God's place as Lord of life.

     I would suggest at the outset that a more
careful reading of this story is called for.

For myself I find it more helpful to think of this passage (as part of the first eleven chapters of Genesis) as the symbolic expression of a deep spiritual truth about the human condition; Adam's story is my story, and it is not less true because it is mythic (which does not mean the same thing as "fairy tale"), but is in fact more true. Be that as it may, I submit that a closer reading of the story reveals that the account of sin as the result of pride does not cut deep enough.

The fundamental thing to note in this story is that the situation within which Adam and Eve become disobedient and assert their desire to be "as God" is one fashioned by the serpent--and it is based on lie! The basic nature of this lie is that God does not want Adam and Eve to eat of the fruit of the tree of the knowledge of good and evil in order to protect God's own superior position, not out of concern for Adam and Eve, not out of concern "lest you die". In short, the serpent tells Adam and Eve that God is threatened by their presence and potential and wants to keep them in their place. It is not surprising that they, in turn, found this defensiveness on God's part threatening to them, and that they became defensive themselves.

Thus, the basis of self-assertive pride is primoridal distrust, based on the assumption that God does not have human well-being as a high priority. It is a well-known psychological fact that defensiveness and aggression arise out of situations in which persons feel threatened, or in which they interpret other persons behavior and/or motivations as threatening. To be sure, it is surprising that Adam and Eve believed the serpent, since they were in a position to know better (to know that God loves and cares for them), but their crucial mistake was a failure to be trustful, which in turn led to defensive self-assertion.

As I understand it, then, the central message of the entire Bible, focused in the "Good News" of the Gospel of Christ, is that what the serpent said was a lie, that God is not threatened by humankind, that God loves us and wants the best for us. At the base of this message of love lies God's forgiveness of our distrustful posture. Not only is God not threatened by our presence and potential, God does not "pick up the marbles and go home" when we behave defensively and pridefully. In Christ God has demonstrated this love and forgiveness; in Christ we can be reconciled to God on the basis of God's unrelenting grace.

Against the backdrop of this understanding of the nature of estrangement and the basis for reconciliation, we are in a better position to interpret the meaning of Christ's work as God's agent of reconciliation. The axial point about which to get perfectly clear is that it is we who are being reconciled to God through the work of Christ, not God. To put this another way, God's love and forgiveness are the basis or cause of Christ's life and work and not the other way around. God was not rendered able to love us becuase of what Christ did, but Christ did what he did because God loves us.

Another important point to stress is that Christ's Incarnation and Atonement are inextricably related to each other, in the sense that his reconciling work is effective because of who he was and how he lived. In other words, he didn't come just to teach or just to die, but he came to live and die in such a way as to reveal the love and grace of God. The Incarnation is God's "cosmic object lesson" or dramatization of the divine nature. In Christ God acts out, in a deeply profound metaphor, who and what God is, how God relates to other beings, how God would be if God were a human and how humans should be toward each other. Divine love (agapé) is at the center of God, as revealed in Christ's life, death, and resurrection--taken as a single, unity event.

The reconciling posture struck by Christ is most pointedly indicated by his radical servant-hood. In spite of the fact that his contempora-ries (and ours!) were incessantly seeking to interpret him in a more dominant role (as political messiah, king, master, etc.) he deliberately cast himself as the suffering servant (baby, teacher, friend, footwasher, etc.) and generally down-played the miraculous aspects of his ministry. In this way God is revealed as the initiator of reconciliation, as the one who takes the risks, who is willing to be vulnerable for our sake. In sum, God is telling us that we do not need to be threatened by divine reality and activity.

This way of looking at the person and work of Christ tends to stress the deliverance and absorption metaphors used for the Atonement in the New Testament and as discussed in Chapter Five. By striking the radical suffering servant posture God, in Christ, undercuts or breaks down or builds bridges over the various barriers of distrust and estrangement that we erect between and among ourselves and God. By taking the "low-ly seat" God, in Christ, bears the cost and the offensive of our distrustful and defensive beha-vior by saying "I love you in spite of the fact that you turn your back on me." In the idiom of human relationships, God is the one who says, "I'm sorry", even when we are the offending party.

Thus, Christ delivers us from the bondage of distrustful and self-centered lives by des-troying the need for such behavior. Christ is the victor over sin and death, which result from defensive, selfish modes of life. In like man-ner, Christ absorbs the venom of hostility which

70

flows from our self-protective and inauthentic
way of being in the world, he takes on himself
the sin and evil generated by our estrangement.
He therefore serves more as our "strong deliver-
er" and as the "lamb of God who bears away the
sin of the world" than as the ransom or payment
made to any angry or holy God. At the same time,
this sacrificial love runs far deeper than subjectivist theories of the Atonement, such as the
Moral Influence Theory, would suggest.

Here, again, it is important to stress that
the central thrust of the New Testament concept
of atonement through the work of Christ is not
the appeasement of God or the insertion of Christ
between us and God's wrath. Rather, it is the
expression and demonstration of God's mercy as
being willing to forgive and overcome the consequences of our "afrontive" behavior toward God.
When the scriptures speak of the "wrath of God"
I believe they are referring to the backside of
God's love, to how we experience God's love when
we do not orient ourselves to it in faith and
trust. When we turn our backs on God the consequences (what Paul calls the "wages of sin") are
estrangement and death, not because God changes
but because we do. Our acceptance of God's grace
enables us to experience divine love as redemptive.

In this light we can now better understand
the meaning of the New Testament teaching concerning "Justification." Rather than focusing
exclusively on a legal interpretation of Christ's
reconciling work, we may now see it in an experiential way. That is, since Christ's work shows
us the depth and constancy of God's forgiveness
and acceptance of us, we have no need of behav-
ing in a defensive manner, of seeking to "justify"
our own existence and worth. Once we grasp the
truely radical nature of this divine love--uncon-
ditional acceptance!--we no longer need to be

justified, since in Christ we are already established in relation to God--and in relation to one another. Our acceptance of this divine acceptance (Paul Tillich's phrase) endows our lives with a powerful and liberating force for redemptive growth. We never again have to worry about our position before God or our own worth - these have been established, justified, in the work of Christ.

It should now be clear that the reconciling work of Christ, the Atonement, involves all aspects of the Christ-event. The quality of his life, as revealed in the Incarnation, is carried through even unto death--he died as he had lived, loving and forgiving--and his resurrection is not a "prize" for having been obedient to some private plan of God, but rather it is the natural outcome of a life lived in faith and trust of God. The resurrection shows that God sustains, stands by, the suffering servant. In this way Christ brings God's mercy to us, in that by identifying ourselves with Christ and incorporating his faithful trust of God into our lives, we, too, participate in divine justification. Christ is _for_ us (Immanuel) because and so that God can be _for_ us.

In conclusion let me add that the foregoing interpretation of the Atonement entails a quite different view from the one most frequently encountered of Christ's words on the cross, "My God, My God. Why have you forsaken me?" This question must not be taken as implying that God had _actually_ forsaken Christ, but rather that in this excruciating trauma, which was spiritual as well as physical, Christ _felt_ forsaken. In fact, the words he used consitute the first verse of _Psalm_ 22, the prayer traditionally uttered by devout Jews at death. The Psalm goes on to acknowledge that God does not forsake the faithful, concluding with an affirmation of trust and con-

72

fidence. This is most likely why Christ chose
the words that he did.

Chapter Ten

Our Humanity: Persons and Less

Once the center of our theological perspective has been located in the person and work of Christ, it does not matter much which order the remaining Christian themes are taken up. Traditionally the doctrine of God's nature is dealt with prior to treating the question of human nature, but since it is our experience of redemption which lies at the center of Christian life and thought it seems fruitful to begin by exploring what that redemptive experience reveals about ourselves. From there we can move on to what it reveals about God.

Our experience of God's reconciling activity can be thought of as having three dimensions; we experience divinity as creator, judge, and redeemer. Therefore our understanding of our own nature can be structured according to these three dimensions. We find ourselves participating in a three-fold, present reality comprised of what theologians frequently call the "created order", the "fallen order", and the "redemptive order". It is important to stress the present reality of each of these orders because far too often they are thought of as periods on a time line, such that the Created Order represents the original human condition, the Fallen Order our present condition, and the Redemptive Order our hope for the future. The New Testament, however, makes it quite clear that we participate in all of these dimensions simultaneously in our present lives.

Christian theology draws a large part of its concept of human nature from the creation story in Genesis, Chapters One through Three. I take this story as a myth in the classic sense of that term (as opposed to its contemporary connotation of "fairytale") because it seeks to explain the perennial human condition rather than to explain our historical beginnings. More pointedly, the creation story describes the shape and dynamic of our human lives as we experience them, laminated as they are with ambiguity and paradox. The New Testament, especially the teachings of Jesus and Paul, reiterates these very same features of our existance, as the following discussion will seek to show.

To begin with, we experience the world and ourselves as having a strong creative, basically good, quality. The created order, which surrounds us and which we partially embody, is that dimension of our reality that speaks of the power and goodness of God, of the divine intentions in creating a world at all. The very fact that the world, and we with it, exists at all necessitates that everything comprising it is in a deep and potential sense good. Chapter One of Genesis reiterates that God regarded all that was made as good (in Hebrew, tov) in the sense that it all fulfilled God's creative purposes. The creation is neither good in and of itself nor good simply because God made it, but it is good instrumentally in relation to God's intentions.

Secondly, we as humans have been created in the image of God. The stress here is not on duplication, but on a structural or functional analogue. One aspect of this analogical relationship is what might be called "unity". As God is one being, although consisting of diverse dimensions, humans are one, unified being as well. In the Old Testament there is clearly no distinction between any inner or outer parts of human nature, such as soul and body. Persons are viewed as holistic, unitary beings. This is essentially the New Testament view as well, though this has been obscured by a strong tendency of theologians throughout Christian history to read the Bible through the dualistic eyes of the classical Greek philosophic

76

mind. The clearest example of this is the confusion in Christendom over the notion of the Immortality of the soul, which is not in any sense a
Biblical doctrine. Rather, it is a Greek notion
standing in sharp contrast to the clear-cut New
Testament teaching of the resurrection of the body.

Other dimensions of the image of God in human
beings include such things as rationality, emotional responses, and volition. In fact, it is in
volitional agency, the experience of choosing that
God's image is most clearly expressed in us. The
capacity for choice is what chiefly characterizes
a being and distinguishes one being from another.
Moreover, in the Judeo-Christian perspective God
is known primarily, if not exclusively, in and
through our interaction with God in personal and
social history, as agent with agent. Another way
of putting this is to say that as humans we are
creatures who have the potential for decision,
commitment, and/or action. We are, in a word,
persons.

In addition it is important not to lose
sight of the social or relational character of the
image of God in human persons. We do not exist before God as isolated individuals, self-contained
atoms, but as part of the common fabric of the
created order. God, too, has this social form of
existence--"Let us make man in our image"--and
thus it is no less crucial in human nature. Indeed, the very capacity to enter into relationship
through action and commitment presupposes a social
millieu within which such agency can take place.
Further, the Old Testament continually stresses
that humans relate to God as the people of God (the
nation of Israel) and the New Testament emphasizes
the church as the body of Christ. Another, and
perhaps the crucial, aspect of the social character
of our nature is found in the centrality of communication through speech. God creates by speaking
("Let there be..."), guides and sustains by speak-

ing ("Hear, oh Israel..."), Christ is regarded as the Word, the church is the body of the "called-out" ones, etc. Linguistic communication is a social, relational phenomenon.

Another main dimension of human nature and experience is that of the fallen Order. At the same time as we experience the goodness of the created order, with all its potential for relationship and communication, we also experience the ambiguities and negativities of what some theologians call the "forces of discreativity." That is, we experience broken relationships, misunderstanding, and evil. This dimension of our humanity is symbolized in the story of the Fall in the third chapter of Genesis. Adam and Eve, through the misuse of their God-given capacity to choose, took up a posture over-against God and thus began to experience God's ever-constant love as judgment, since they were out of harmony with it. In this basic choice we as humans express our lack of trust in God (or our self-trust) and bring upon ourselves the natural consequences thereof.

In this judgmental or fallen dimension of experience all of the potentialities of the created order are subject to distortion and abusement, biblically termed "sin." Some theologians, such as Calvin, have gone so far as to say that the image of God in humans is destroyed by sin, but the scriptures do not bear this interpretation out. In addition, it is important not to locate the source of sin in reason or our bodies, or some other aspect of our nature, thereby implying that it is evil in itself or has become essentially evil. The scriptures characterize sin as a relational quality stemming from a choice to ignore one's creature-hood and based in a lack of trust. The results of this choice are to instill in us the possibility, indeed the propensity, to abuse our God-given capacities and to subject us to the consequences thereof ("to stew in our own juice", as it were) the ultimate one being death.

It is especially important to expand on this point a bit. The implications that follow from a solid understanding of the social and relational quality of our human existence are extremely significant. This way of being in the world entails a relational value system such that the criterion for moral worth is the establishment and development of relationships which are productive of high quality human life. Likewise, the criterion for judging any form of human conduct as evil, or sinful, is the extent to which it debilitates and limits the quality of human relationships. Even the direct ethical teachings of the Judeo-Christian faith, such as the Ten Commandments and The Sermon on The Mount, are presented, not as arbitrary ends-in-themselves, given by God for their own sake, but as the means whereby human life will be more meaningful and rich. Evil is thus a function of disrelationship.

The tendency to equate evil and sin with our bodily existence is especially strong as a result of our inherited Greek, dualistic perspective. In the biblical view embodied existence is part of the created order and in this sense "good". In the fallen order it is subject to misuse, but this does not render it essentially sinful. All that is necessary to avoid this confusion is to recall that Christ himself took on bodily form in the Incarnation ("became flesh") and that the Christian hope of resurrection centers in the body, as Christ's resurrection clearly illustrates. The scriptures affirm that our body is a vital aspect of our personhood, whether in its positive or negative expression. This is why Paul exhorts us "to present our bodies as a living sacrifice" (Romans 12:1,2).

This point about the importance of our embodiment to our basic human nature warrants special underlining. This is particularly true with respect to the sexuality dimension of our existence.

79

At least since Augustine, Christians generally have been embarrased about sexuality and the role it does or does not play in Christian values. Fortunately, the scriptures do not share in this embarrasment, speaking forthrightly about sexual matters. In fact, the most fundamental verb used to depict the nature of the proper relationship of the nation Israel to God in the Old Testament is that designating sexual intercourse.

In coming to a healthy understanding of the human condition we need liberating from both the puritan and the playboy philosophy. We _are_ bodies and our sexuality participates in the goodness of the created order as well as in the distortion of the fallen order (_and_ in the restoration of the redemptive order). We also need liberating from the male "sexism" that for too long has dominated both Western culture and the Christian church. I shall return to this theme at the close of the next chapter.

Another important distinction to draw when discussing our life within the fallen order is that between original _sin_ and original _guilt_. From the biblical emphasis on our participation in sin from "square one", as represented in the story of Adam and Eve, it does not follow that we are guilty or responsible for our sin before we ever get started. Evil is in the world, as both a reality and a potentiality, as and when we enter it. We are contaminated by it and participate in it without being responsible for its existence. We _are_, however, responsible for our _own_ participation in it. In no sense are we held responsible for a decision made by previous persons, whether an historical Adam and Eve or our parents, though we clearly experience the fruits both positive and negative, of their decisions.

Another way to come at this whole question is to explore the social character of sin. Far too

80

often Christians have tended to think of sin as a strictly individual matter, wherein each person is fully and only responsible for their own sinful posture. One result of this way of thinking is the idea that if we just straighten out each individual's relationship with God, we shall thereby do away with evil. But this approach ignores the social, corporate nature of human existence. We are not simply a collection of individuals, but rather we are an organic body, or a woven fabric, in which the consequences of any one member's actions are shared by all, for good or ill. Moreover, since sin is essentially a matter of relationship, the more we compound our society, the more complex its relationships become, thus the more we multiply and intensify evil. This fact has led some theologians to maintain that it is impossible to forge a viable connection between the Christian ethic of love, which is applicable on the individual level, and socio-political policy on the group level, as we saw in Chapter Six. In short, there is such a thing as "institutional" racism, sexism, age-ism, etc.

The third main dimension of human existence is that of the redemptive order. Just as all things (including humans) were created good, according to God's purpose, and all things participating in the distortion of good, on the basis of choice, just so nothing lies outside of the redemptive potential of God's activity in Christ. This does not necessarily imply that everyone will, in fact, be redeemed, or that God is in absolute control of the fate of all person. It does imply, however, that the only thing that can keep a person from participating in God's redemptive activity is the individual's refusal to do so. For God can make good come out of every situation if those who are involved co-operate with divine love (Romans 8:28).

The means by which we participate in the redemptive order is a dynamic process involving several cyclical phases. The first phase, the crucial one, is that whereby we initially identify ourselves with Christ, his life, death, and resurrection. This is more than a simple pledge of allegiance or resolution. It is, rather, a mystery in which we are actually united with Christ and which is symbolized by Baptism and Holy Communion. As we open ourselves to him, he opens himself to us. The second phase of the redemptive process is confessing our tendency to live apart from God and availing ourselves of divine forgiveness. Thirdly, through God's forgiving grace we allow ourselves to be redirected toward life in the Spirit. Fourthly, we acknowledge our acceptance of the consequences of, or judgment for, our sin.

This is a cyclical process in the sense that it must be repeated over and over again as we continue in the Christian life. The reason this repetition is necessary is that redemption is a growth process which begins when we identify ourselves with Christ and will only be culminated "in that day when he will make all things new." Being a Christian does not mean taking on a whole new character all at once--though the full potential has been provided. Nonetheless, the continual participation in the redemptive cycle will gradually bear fruit in the lives and dispositions of those who avail themselves of it.

In conclusion it is well to remind ourselves once again of the corporate nature of our existence, especially as it relates to our experience of the redemptive order. Just as our participation in the goodness of creation and the judgment of evil is mediated in and through our relationships with other persons, on both the individual and socio-political levels, so our experience of redemption comes in and through our involvement in the community of those who share in God's grace. Christians together constitute the body of Christ and thereby support and nourish one another. Of course, the Christian community must not be equated with those socio-economic institutions known as churches or denominations. Nor are the two to be thought of as mutually exclusive. The biblical term "the Church" denotes all those who participate in the ongoing life of Christ, a good number of whom may well belong to various organized churches and others of whom may not. In any case, it is the shared life of the corporate Christian community through which redemption is actualized.

Chapter Eleven

God's Character: Sovereign and More

As we have seen, Christ's Incarnation and Atonement reveal as much about our humanity as they do about his personhood. In like fashion, they reveal to us the central motifs of God's character as well. Our examination of our experience of reconciliation of Christ brought to light the creative, judgmental, and redemptive aspects of God's personhood. In this chapter we shall examine even more closely Christ's reconciling activity to see what it tells us about God's character.

The most important feature is likely to be the one we shall overlook, partly because it is so familiar and partly because its radical quality so often goes unappreciated. I am speaking here of the fact that at the heart of the Christian gospel stands God's <u>activity.</u> God <u>did</u> something in our world and in our history. When compared, on the one hand, to the conception of God in other major religions or, on the other hand, to that of traditional philosophies, the Judeo-Christian idea of divinity is quite remarkable because it does not depict God as a static, totally transcendent being or as the very "Ground of Being" itself. In the Christian faith, divinity is not abstract, but concrete; God is the God who <u>acts</u>.

There are several aspects of this notion of an active God which warrant unpacking. The first is quite simply that God is presented in the scriptures as an <u>agent</u>. This is what is meant by all of the anthropomorphic ways of speaking about God which focus divine personhood. It is natural to speak of divinity in terms appropriate to persons because we experience God through interaction with the religious dimension of our existence. God acts in our world and lives, we respond and our history unfolds according to this reciprocal pattern of action and interaction. God is one with whom we interrelate. This notion of interrelation, wherein God initiates action, makes promises, and expresses concern for humanity, stands in marked contrast to those conceptions of God, such as that of the ancient Greeks, in which God was thought of as alternatively indifferent to or in total control of human lives.

Here again it needs to be emphasized that in the Judeo-Christian view our most important understanding of divinity begins with our involvement with God in our concrete historical existence. Although we may have a general conception of God (from nature and morality) which is filled-in and made specific by revelation, it is through our interaction with Christ that we come to experience God's reconciling love and to form a concrete conception of divine character. Thus all of our theology must be grounded in that historical and existential experience as shared through history, community, and personal involvement.

A second important theme entailed in the notion of divinity as active agent is that God is the initiator of our reconciliation. As the opening verse of Genesis has it, "In the beginning God ..." Or as Paul puts it, "While we were yet sinners, Christ died for us." Once again the contrast with other conceptions of God is striking. The Judeo-Christian God does not sit aloof, waiting to be appeased by the sacrifices and obedience of humankind. Rather, the Christian God initiates creative and redemptive activity on our behalf for the purpose of establishing an enriching relationship between divinity and humanity. This pattern is revealed in both the Old Testament, where in Exodus God's deliverance precedes the people's

86

commitment and the giving of the law, and in the New Testament, where we are told that God loves humankind in such a way as to <u>give</u> Christ as the first move in the redemptive process. (<u>John</u> 3:16)

A third theme which flows from the above two pertains to the special implications of the notion of incarnation. For, this notion stresses the <u>enfleshment</u> of divinity, God's actual becoming flesh as a means of effecting reconciliation. The positive side of this enfleshment is that by this act God sanctifies the human way of being-in-the-world. This counteracts the tendency, found both in the traditional Greek and in the Oriental way of thought, to think of the body as a source of evil and/or a hindrance to the pursuit of truth and goodness. The negative side of this act is that Christ gave up many divine prerogatives when he became human. Christ did not merely <u>appear</u> to be human, but actually became subject to the limitations and temptations of embodied existence. And yet, within these parameters, he lived a life totally given to God and thereby accomplished our redemption.

The basic characteristic of God focused by the foregoing themes is that of love. Now, many pens have run dry trying to define divine love, and I am not going to add mine to the list. Nevertheless, a few of its crucial dimensions are clearly revealed in the Incarnation and Atonement, and it is important to discuss them at least briefly here. The first is manifest by the fact that God's reconciling work in Christ is a <u>gift</u>. This tells us that God's love is a giving love. This means that it is neither earned nor based on any prerequisite conditions. God's love is given freely and unconditionally. Moreover, it is bestowed in spite of and in order to overcome our chosen estrangement from God.

87

The Greek term used in the New Testament for
love (agapĕ) denotes an active concern for the
basic or ultimate well-being of others without
consideration of merit or consequences. This is
the central thrust of the Christian concept of
God. Part of the meaning here is to give what
is needed, not necessarily what is wanted. The
Good Samaritan provides an especially fine example of Christian love because he acts according
to the needs of the man he found in the ditch.
Another part of the meaning of agapĕ love is the
notion of servanthood and/or sacrifice. Divine
love is costly in the sense that it involves the
giving of what is most dear to God and thereby
placing God in a most vulnerable position, since
some will inevitably reject the gift.

One other prominent characteristic of God's
love needs to be mentioned, namely that it is a
forgiving love. It is this basic ground of forgiveness which provides the foundation for the
New Testament notions of "Justification" and
Righteousness". Divine "rightness" and glory are
not based in having God's demands met, but in
God's ability to forgive and to accept humans
simply as they are as persons and less. This
radical acceptance is difficult for us to understand since we are conditioned to think that "no
one over gets something for nothing." The gift
of forgiveness is grounded in nothing but God's
own loving character. This divine acceptance is
also difficult for us to accept, thus we are always trying to earn God's pleasure by being "good
and decent people." We shall take up this tendency to put the cart before the horse more
thoroughly in Chapter Twelve.

God's forgiving love provides our justification, not because it makes us worthy, but because it sets aside the whole question of worth.
We are accepted in Christ because he absorbs the
evil forces that bind us and renders our guilt a

nonsequitor. We are justified if we choose to
participate in the life, death, and resurrection
of Christ because this is God's way of demonstra-
ting divine forgiveness. This is what Paul means
in the first chapter of Romans when he says that
the righteousness of God is revealed in the gospel of Christ "through faith for faith." All
that is necessary for us to be justified is our
acceptance by faith of God's forgiveness made concrete in Christ. This act of commitment renders
irrelevant all human attempts at self-justifica-
tion, whether by keeping the Old Testament law or
by doing good works to prove our faith. In the
end it is God's grace and this grace alone that
reconciles us to God, to ourselves, and to one
another.

In the foregoing discussion I sought to unpack the more important features of the notion of
God as an active being, as embodied in Christ's
Incarnation and Atonement. It remains for us to
summarize briefly some of the other characteristics of God's personhood which are arrived at by
more indirect means. In this regard it is important once again to remind ourselves that theology
is strictly a human enterprise and at best deals
in analogies and approximations. The characteristics of God suggested on the following pages
represent an attempt to distill some insights
from the overall record of God's activity in
history, especially as presented in the scripture.

First off, there are what might be called
the more "personal" divine characteristics. God
is known as the creator, both because God is the
source of the cosmos and because God is experienced as the source of creativity in the lives of
those who commit themselves. The same line of
reasoning holds for such traditional, personal
characteristics as God's power (omnipotence),
wisdom (omniscience), and constant presence
(omnipresence). God has been experienced as such

in the concrete history of countless thousands of people from the time of Abraham down to the present, therefore their theological efforts have converged to define God in these terms. Many of these characteristics have been focused in certain main images, such as that of Father and that of King, both of which seek to stress the providential quality of God's relation to humankind.

Another set of personal characteristics cluster around more moral or inner qualities, such as spirituality, comfort-giving, and integrity. Many of these pertain to what have traditionally been called feminine and/or motherly traits, and they are focused in the person of the Holy Spirit in the New Testament. Jesus, too, displayed an essentially androgynous character when he openly expressed his needs, wept, assumed the role of servant, and exuded tenderness (see especially the passage where he likens himself to a mother hen who would gather Jerusalem under her wings). Interestingly enough, the creation story in Genesis speaks of God in the plural ("Let us make humankind in our image"); and we were created male and female; and several times the feminine gender is used when referring to God's spirit in the Old Testament.

The quality of integrity merits special attention. Throughout the scriptures God's claim to our allegiance never rests simply on divine authority as creator and sustainer of the cosmos and/or human life. Rather it is continually anchored in the quality of God's character and love, and in particular in divine integrity. God is presented as a maker and keeper of promises, as the God of Abraham, Isaac, and Jacob, as the offended party in a covenant with Israel, as the promiser and sender of the Messiah, as the Father of our Lord Jesus Christ who will return again, fulfilling and renewing all creation. Because of having entered into relationship with humankind in time and place, God is able to make promises and is willing to be held accountable for those which are made. Because God has been faithful in the past, we are warranted in placing our trust in God for the future. This is the line of reasoning offered by the scriptures: God is trustworthy because God proves faithful.

There are also some more "official" or theoretic sorts of characteristics which are traditionally ascribed to God by theologians. One of these is summarized in the doctrine of the Trinity. There is no specific biblical basis for the doctrine of the trinity. It is, strictly speaking, an inferential notion drawn from the fact that in the New Testament God the Father, Christ the Son, and the Holy Spirit all seem to be spoken of as divine and yet monotheism is still maintained. Throughout Christian history various explanations of this paradoxical trinitarian doctrine have been offered. Some have suggested the idea of One God who is expressed in three modes, while others have proposed that the God-head is more like a committee composed of three members, each of whom is in a sense God, but not exhaustively so. Much of the force of the notion of the trinity comes from personal Christian experience in which God seems to be interacting with us in (at least) three main ways, (1) as creator, sustainer and judge, (2) as friend and redeemer, and (3) as convictor and comforter.

Although this is both a helpful and a difficult doctrine, it is crucial to bear in mind that it does not lie near the center of Christian revelation in the sense that it is entailed by the Incarnation and/or Atonement. The pivotal thing we need to know--and experience--about God is not the inner psychology of the divine being, which will always remain an essential mystery to us in any case. What we need to know is that God is an active, loving being who has entered into our historical experience on our behalf even though we often do not reciprocate. For myself, I favor the explanation which sees <u>God as a relationship</u> amongst three separate volitional centers who are by choice of a unified mind and purpose, and who act in concert.

Another "official" or theoretic doctrine about God which has often been at the forefront theologically is that of sovereignty. The standard "reformed" notion of sovereignty flows out of the thought of John Calvin. The stress in Calvin's work is on the absolute, unilateral power and authority of God in all matters, including human redemption. Thus he taught that not only is salvation a gift, but the very capacity to receive it, namely faith, is also a gift of God. Thus he developed a strong doctrine of election in which some are elected to salvation and some are not, the basis of the choice being hidden in the arbitrary, but loving will of God. Calvin argued that to in any way share the responsibility for their own redemption with humankind necessarily detracts from the sovereignty and thus from the glory of God.

My own reading of the scripture will not support this view. The constant emphasis on and urging to faith, the agonizing struggle of Christ in the garden over whether or not to do the Father's will, and the very significance of the Incarnation and Atonement all point in the opposite direction. As I see it, once God chose to create human beings--persons with whom one could enter into meaningful relationships of trust and love--God also chose a self-limitation, setting aside total control of the world. Perhaps a helpful example here might be the case of parents who may well be sovereign in deciding whether or not to have children, but once they have them they have relinquished that sovereignty in order to achieve the potential of a higher end. Thus it is more praiseworthy of God, not to maintain absolute sovereignty but to say God is willing to sacrifice some divine prerogatives for the sake of humankind and God's own creative power. God is sovereign and _more_!

This same point can be seen in the pattern of Incarnation and Atonement. The whole purpose of the redemptive activity of God taking the specific form that it does is to emphasize the willingness of God not to be in absolute control of human destiny. Divinity came to humankind in their own terms--place, time, language, etc.-- offering love, becoming vulnerable to rejection. God's power does not lie in being able to control the outcome of every situation but in the _quality_ of God's involvement _in_ every situation. The nature of trust and love in a relationship require freedom·of choice on the part of the beloved. A gift is not a gift if it cannot be rejected. God has chosen to be _more_ than sovereign by being _less_, in the sense of entering into an interpersonal relation with those who believe.

A final note. Remembering that the terms we use for describing divine reality are in the final analysis human metaphors (this is both their strength and their limitation), I would suggest that we must acknowledge the historical and cultural limitations of our tradition of speaking of God exclusively in masculine terms. It is important to think of God in concrete and personal images (as contrasted to abstract and impersonal ones), such as King, Father, and Shepherd, but it is also important not to miss out on the many other dimensions of God's character that can be expressed in additional images, including those traditionally associated with feminine aspects of human experience. We must be careful neither to limit our understanding of God nor our appreciation of half of the human race by chosing exclusively masculine images for God's character. By

varying our images, where appropriate, we en-
richen our theology and our shared lives,
as well.

Chapter Twelve

Embodied Love: Gift or Duty?

The consideration of Christian ethical responsibility flows naturally from many of the
concerns of the foregoing chapters. The central
thrust of God's redemptive activity in Christ's
Incarnation and Atonement not only reveals the
basic character of humanity and of God, but it
calls for a response on our part as well. This
response involves the living a life of love, to
follow the example and commandment of Christ, to
love God with all our being and our neighbor as
we do ourselves. The Christian's responsibility
is to embody God's love.

The first point that needs to be made is
that the Christian ethic is based on and in gratitude. Thus the sense in which it is a responsibility needs to be clarified at the outset.
Although it is not entirely misleading to speak
of the Christian commandment and duty to love,
it is imperative to understand that Christian
ethical responsibility is not a requirement in
the sense of a prerequisite or condition for participating in redemption. Rather, it is the expression of gratitude for benefits already received. As Paul points out in Romans 12:1 and 2,
on the basis of the mercies of God (as presented
in the first eleven chapters of Romans) we are
urged (beseeched), not commanded, to present ourselves for sacrificial Christian living. It is
a responsibility in the sense that it is an appropriate response to the redemptive activity of
God.

This same pattern is seen in the book of
Exodus in the Old Testament. It is essential
to note that the book does not begin with the

95

Ten Commandments; they come in the twentieth chapter. The book begins, as does Romans, with an account of human need. Next, it moves to the activity of God on behalf of humankind, followed by a commitment of faith on the part of the people to become God's people. This same logic characterized Paul's thought in his letter to the Christians at Rome. When this pattern has become a reality in the divine-human relationship, then (and only then) is it appropriate to speak of Christian ethical responsibility. In Exodus the Ten Commandments were given as a guide to the expression of gratitude and faith for a people who had already been delivered by and who had already committed themselves to God. The same holds true in the New Testament teaching.

Another way to make this point clear is to focus on the very common biblical image of fruit. This image is focused very powerfully in Galatians where Paul speaks of Christian ethical responsibility as expressing itself in the "fruit of the Spirit." Perhaps the most obvious thing about fruit--and one which often goes unnoticed--is that it flows naturally and inevitably from a healthy vine or tree. Fruit cannot be commanded or attached from the outside, it must come from the inside of its own accord. The farmer's job is to see to it that the conditions for a healthy vine are provided and then to trust the God-ordained natural processes. How much grief would Christian parents and teachers save themselves and others if they could really understand this!

The purpose of producing fruits of the Spirit, of embodying Christian love, is to become a means of sharing God's redemptive activity with others. It is not a way of earning salvation, or of accumulating "brownie points" with God. So often we hear it said that in the Old Testament times people were saved by obeying the Ten Commandments, while in the New Testament times people

are saved by faith alone. Nothing could be more
unbiblical. No one was ever saved by keeping the
commandments, number one because it is beyond our
present human capacities, and number two, they
were not given for this purpose, as we've already
seen. People are made whole by entering into a
relationship of trust with a loving God. They
embody and express this trust by seeking to be
like God as an expression of gratitude and as a
means of sharing God's love with others.

Another basic feature of the Incarnation and
Atonement that bears on our understanding of the
Christian ethic pertains to the activity focus
which characterizes God's love in Christ. The
New Testament term for divine love (agapē) does
not designate an emotion, but rather a kind of
action. As was pointed out earlier on, the emphasis is on how (the manner in which) God loves,
not on the degree of God's feeling--"God loved
the world so as to give His only son..." Thus
the love Christians seek to share must be of the
same nature. This is not to say that emotional
love is unrelated to the Christian ethic, but it
is important to see that the feeling of love and
the activity of loving are not necessarily the
same thing. There will be times when our duty
to love requires us to go beyond the limits of
our emotional range, as indeed the Good Samaritan
did; he loved the man in the ditch by actively
meeting his needs in spite of his dislike for
Jews.

This point can be made from a slightly different angle by considering the fact that Christians are urged and commanded to love others, and
emotions are not subject to such modes of speech.
Emotions cannot be turned on or off at will, but
rather grow out of the natural conditions provided by personality, conditioning, and circumstances. To be sure, in time these factors can
to a large degree be shaped so as to form a lov-

ing disposition. In the meantime, however, we must express God's love by our actions whether or not we feel the corresponding emotion. Ultimately it is psychologically impossible--and irrelevant--to be able to feel compassion for everyone, but it is possible to seek to behave toward others in ways which facilitate their ultimate well-being.

The more positive side of this New Testament emphasis on the active character of Christian love is focused forcefully in that pivotal passage in Romans, Chapter Twelve, verses 1 and 2. To begin with, note that Paul does not say that the appropriate response to God's mercies is to commit one's soul or spirit to God. Rather, he urges us to "present our bodies" as a living sacrifice. Contrary to popular Christian opinion, the New Testament does not teach that humans have souls which are immortal, encased in bodies which are somehow evil and destined for ultimate corruption. It teaches, rather, that humans are unified persons comprised of both spirit and flesh which in combination are referred to as either "the soul" or "the body". Thus Paul urges us to commit our whole selves so as to be able to serve God by the way we live, that is, by our activity.

The extension of Christian love is totally inclusive. By this I mean that Christians have a responsibility to extend and express God's love to all persons without qualification. The personal dimension of this inclusiveness is dramatized by Jesus' story of the Good Samaritan. When he stressed the importance of loving one's neighbor and was asked "Who is my neighbor?", Jesus reversed the thrust of the question by focusing on a person who acted "neighborly" without trying to distinguish between a neighbor and a non-neighbor. In fact, a major factor in the story is the Samaritan's willingness to cut across hostile religious and racial lines to do the loving thing. In another place Jesus gets more explicit when he says that we are to love our enemies. He backed this teaching up in his own life when he asked God to forgive those who were crucifying him.

The social dimension of the inclusiveness of Christian love is seen most clearly in Paul's teaching wherein he insists that in Christ, or from Christ's perspective, there exist no essential distinctions between Jew and Gentile, slave and master, male and female. This teaching directly contradicts the daily prayer of the devout Jewish male, in which he thanked God that he was born neither Gentile, nor slave, nor female. One of the great dramas of the New Testament, especially of the book of The Acts of The Apostles, is the struggle which Paul and the early church went through in coming to grips with this truth. Although they did not always perfectly embody the inclusive love of Christ, they did propose it as an ideal and grew toward it. Paul's acknowledgment of the importance of specific women in the churches he founded, visited, and corresponded with, together with his attack on the legalistic Jewish Christians and his instructions concerning the treatment of slaves, all make this abundantly clear. The gospel of love stands opposed to all exclusiveness and oppression.

Finally, let us return to the question focused in Chapter Six concerning the relevance and practicality of the Christian ideal of absolute love. My own position on this issue is two-fold. First, I do think that the ideal of perfect love is unrealizable, and that for two reasons. To begin with, the redemptive process in which we participate in Christ begins here and now but will not be completed until God makes all things new. Thus we are living a mixed or ambiguous existence during which we grow toward the ideal by appropriating God's grace in Christ, but also during which we are never completely freed from the influence of "the flesh, the world, and the devil." At the same time many, if not most, of the people in the world do not participate in the redemptive process and yet we must live in commonality with them. Thus our social mode of existence will of necessity involve us in compromise and choosing the least evil amongst various alternatives.

The above realities render the connection between the Christian ideal of love and our socio-political existence very complicated at best. Thus it is that the notion of justice, as defined and implemented by humans, becomes a necessity. The closest we can come to perfect love in a world marred by evil and limitation is a human-istic form of justice. Although it is more difficult to administer and less "efficient" in the short run, a democratic and constitutional government would seem to be as Winston Churchill put it, "the worst form of government, except for all the rest." Or to quote Reinhold Niebuhr, "It is our capacity for goodness which makes democracy possible and our capacity for evil which makes it necessary."

Second, although the ideal of perfect love is unrealizable, it in nowise follows that it is impractical. On the contrary, I am convinced that such an ideal is of inestimable value, and that for two reasons. As we live in the Christian life we are continually reminded by the absolute standard of love that we fall short. The awareness of this judgment fosters both confession and reliance on God's grace, thereby freeing us from the illusion that we are self-sufficient. Such humility is of great worth, both because it is realistic and because it is a prerequisite to receiving God's grace. Also, the absolute ideal of love continually serves as a challenge to us to grow towards actualizing it more and more fully. It gives us a concrete goal toward which to work and provides the means by which our growth becomes possible.

Perhaps this two-fold and seemingly paradoxical position on the relevancy of an unrealizable ideal can be illustrated and substantiated by applying it to the question of pacifism. On the one side stand those who affirm the use of force (including war, capital punishment, and self-defense) as ethically proper for Christians. They maintain that the ideal of perfect love is unrealizable and thus impractical for our time and place. On the other side stand those who deny the use of force as a viable Christian alternative. These maintain that the ideal of perfect love is applicable to the present human situation and that any compromise with it is unethical from a Christian point of view. Finally, there are those who deny the inherent rightness or goodness of force, but at the same time acknowledge that given the world we live in the refusal to use force often results in more evil than the use of it. In such cases one does not claim to have done "the good" thing but "the appropriate" thing or the necessary thing, the lesser of two evils. Here, as always, one acts with contrition, relying on the forgiveness and grace of God.

Thus, the Christian ethic of embodied love, reflecting as it does an incarnational reality, must be both concrete and flexible. It must not confuse love with sentimentality on the one hand, nor with conventional morality on the other hand. Hard choices have to be made, the ideal must be approximated, and contrition is always in order. Yet, as Luther said, because we must act, nonetheless always within the fallen order, we must act, and thus sin, "boldly." We are called to embody responsible love, not to be morally pure. This is another way of saying that the Christian ethic is an ethic of the Spirit, not one of the letter. As Jesus himself said, "The Sabbath (as all law) is made to facilitate human well-being, not the other way around."

To return to our discussion of human nature in Chapter Ten, it is the quality of human relationship, both with God and with others, that serves as the criterion of value in ethical considerations. The laws God gives or that we make are meant to and only function well when they do, serve the ultimate well-being of humankind. It is, of course, easy to rationalize our way around a lot of moral responsibilities by abusing this principle. But no truth is beyond abuse, and it is also easy to put strictures on God's love and poison human life in the name of high-sounding, self-serving "morality."

It should be clear by now that I see the Christian ethic of love as an exceedingly radical proposal. It must not be allowed to degenerate into traditional cultural mores and legalism--and it must always be more "hardnosed" than a simplistic "situational ethic" would imply. It calls for nothing less than a radical giving away of self in servanthood to others, not in a wishy-washy, spineless self-humiliation, but in the strong and humanizing way bodied-forth by Christ himself. God came as a servant, and Christians can do no less--and certainly we can do no more. Such a love is unconditional--God loved us in Christ while we were yet sinners--and is exceedingly costly--look what it cost God! We are called to open ourselves to others in the same way that God opened divine mercy and grace to us.

Chapter Thirteen

Christian Scriptures: Sources and Resources

At first it may seem like a long way from the Incarnation and Atonement--God's redemptive activity in Christ--to a doctrine of the authority of the Judeo-Christian scriptures. I trust, however, that the organic connection between the two will become evident as the discussion progresses. Once again I am convinced that so much of the controversy over how to understand and use the scriptures stems from the fact that theologians frequently begin from an arbitrary and/or deductive starting place which runs counter to the central thrust of the Gospel. So rather than pick and choose between and amongst the standard "objectivist" and "subjectivist" views outlined in Chapter One, I shall seek to follow a more Incarnational approach.

To begin with, the Judeo-Christian scriptures can be said to reflect the same general Incarnational character as God's activity among humankind, since they are historical and mediated in character. Their <u>historical</u> character is reflected in the fact that they originated in and span a specific period of human history, and are thus inextricably bound up with specific events, people, and places. The Judeo-Christian scriptures are not simply a collection of profound sayings and teachings, but are rather a compendium of accounts of important <u>doings</u> which mediate certain truths about God and humankind. They have a public, social quality and texture to them which render them both "earthy" and spiritual at the same time.

The theological significance of this historical character lies in the fact that it reveals

God's concern for concrete human existence as lived. God takes human life, with all of its limitations and ambiguities, seriously enough to enter into it and work for its ultimate fulfillment. In the same way, the scriptures arise out of and show a sensitivity to the diverse and solid dimensions of human reality, while at the same time providing a way which leads to their completion and transcendence. The variety of literary forms in the scriptures--story, history, prayers, religious instructions, songs, letters, apocalyptic literature, etc.--and the different languages--Hebrew, Aramaic, and Greek-all testify to the Incarnational character of the scriptures. Moreover, the wide variety of authors and the unpretentious quality of their writing provide additional anchorage in the historical dimension of human experience. Whatever truths are presented in the scripture, they are incarnated in the languages, times, places, and persons of human existence in the world.

The above way of puttings things leads directly into a consideration of the mediated character of the Judeo-Christian scriptures. The fact is that the scriptures did not drop from heaven in a hermetically sealed bag, untouched by human hands, but arose from within a community of real people in actual times and places in order to express and meet concrete human needs; this fact carries with it the implication that the truth and authority of the scriptures is not direct but indirect in character. This mediated mode of communication is of a piece with the open-yet-veiled quality of God's revelation in the Incarnated Christ. As Paul puts it, "Now we see through a glass, darkly..." adequately for our needs, but not fully. Neither the Incarnation nor the scriptures provides a direct communication of God's activity in the human sphere, but both provide a mediated yet sufficient presentation of it.

Theologically this mediated character of the
scriptures means that they cannot be looked to as
an infallible guide in all matters. They may
well serve as the primary authority for faith and
life, but not as the only authority. The accounts
and insights provided by the authors of scripture
are the mediators of divine truth as revealed in
God's activity in the life of Israel and in the
life of Christ. But as mediators they continually
stand in need of interpretation by the Christian
community in each ensuing age and in divergent
locales. All communication is meaningful only
with a concrete context of physical, historical,
and social reality.

The scriptures derive their authority from
the fact that they arose in the immediate wake
of God's activity in our world. This does not
make them infallible nor beyond interpretation,
but it does render them crucial and even primary
sources for Christian living and theological effort. Even as God's self-revelation in history
is veiled sufficiently to allow humans existential space within which to express their freedom
and sincerity, so too the scriptural reflection
upon that revelation is mediated in and through
history and circumstances in order to preserve
the need for human involvement. The Christian
community and the individual Christian must work
together in and around the scripture in order to
discern God's revelation in each time and place.

From all of this it follows that the scriptures are authoritative within the Christian
community because they function as our primary
sources or means of access to God's historical
self-revelation. It will be helpful to trace
briefly the manner in which the various parts
of the scripture serve in this way. For convenience, but to vastly over-simplify, let us consider in turn the Old Testament, the Gospels,

and the activities of the young church as re-
corded in the Acts of The Apostles and the letters of the New Testament.

The Old Testament functions as a source for
Christian life and thought by documenting what
might be called the external and internal life of
that community which provides the seed-plot within which the reconciling activity of God in Christ
takes its roots and from which it draws much of
its meaning. It is the nation Israel which provides the people, time, place, and much of the
symbolism comprising the background against which
the message of the New Testament takes on significance. Moreover, it is in the Old Testament
that the essence of that message is introduced
and developed far more thoroughly than modern
Christians realize. The main "New Testament"
themes of human need, God's character and active
self-revelation in history, and the responsibility to share God's love with others (including
the oppressed and the enemy) are all central to
most of the Old Testament.

Much of the authority of the Old Testament
account of the external life of the Hebrew nation
derives from its historical accuracy and insight
as established by archaeological research. Within the last fifty years hundreds of explorations
have uncovered thousands of documents which cast
direct light upon the significance of many Old
Testament passages and events, and which establish the general validity of its account of the
interactions of the Hebrews with other civiliza-
tions. More specifically the discovery of the
Qumran scrolls takes our knowledge of the text of
the Old Testament back two thousand years, pre-
dating the birth of Christ. Their corroboration
of our more recent Old Testament manuscripts
lends increased authority to the claim that they
themselves are reliable records of the actual
history of the Hebrews.

The authority of the Old Testament's account of the internal life of Israel resides primarily in the existential authenticity and insight with which the literature abounds. The development of individual and national moral character, the realistic presentation of both the assets and liabilities of God's "chosen people", and the general wisdom which characterizes the Hebrew mode of existence all work together to give the Old Testament an authoritative ring. Also there is the rising consciousness of the Hebrews concerning the inclusive character of God's love and of the importance of sacrificial servanthood as a means of effecting redemption--for both the nation and God.

The Gospels derive their authority from the diverse yet essentially unified way in which they mediate·the life and death of Jesus Christ. Despite their brevity and differences the gospel accounts manage to present the person of Christ in a most forceful and compelling manner. Thus they serve as our primary sources of knowledge about the crucial agent of God's reconciling activity. Their authority does not reside in any full, consistent account of the exact movements and/or inner thoughts of Jesus. This sense of the "historical Jesus" is too flat to catch his true significance. Nor does their authority lie solely in the heightened "self-understanding" that results from our authentic interaction with the stories of Jesus' doings and sayings. To overly symbolize the Gospels is to deny their incarnational character.

To my mind the authority of the Gospels comes from the fact that the simple accounts of Jesus' mode of being-in-the-world, as manifested in his interactions with other persons, mediate the redemptive and reconciling activity of God on humanity's behalf. It is primarily in what has been called the "speech-events" of Jesus in dialogue with various individuals and groups

107

that engage and challenge the hearer to participate in God's redemptive activity. The nature of
these speech-events is particularly well focused
in Jesus' use of parables, which reveal truth
about both the speaker and the hearer, but only
indirectly. They demand our involvement while
providing room for our freedom.

The activities of the early church as portrayed in the book of Acts and the New Testament
letters provide yet a third dimension to scriptural authority, drawing it from the fact that the
experiences of the first Christian community function as a paradigm for the church in all ages and
places. This paradigmatic role does not render
the particulars of the New Testament church manda-
tory for all times and places, but it does give a
general shape and direction for others to follow.
Furthermore, the particular interpretation of God's
reconciling activity in Christ given by the Apostles, especially Paul, need not be infallible in
order to be authoritative and helpful. As Paul
himself puts it, "All scripture is inspired by God
and is profitable...that the man of God may be
complete, equipped for every good work."

This quotation, from Paul's second letter to
Timothy, brings us to the second way in which the
scriptures serve as the standard within the Christian Community, namely as a primary resource for
guiding life and thought. It is important to bear
in mind that the scriptures are not some sort of
divine "Ouigie board" whereby one can find God's
advice for the day. To use the Bible as a spiritual "decoder"--whether for personal guidance or
for prophetic prognostications--is to disregard
completely its incarnational character and genius.
The proper use of the scripture as a resource for
personal Christian living depends upon a basic
knowledge of the historical and literary principles involved, as well as upon a sensitivity to

the Bible as a whole and the guidance of the Holy Spirit. This does <u>not</u> imply that one needs to be a preacher or theological specialist to interpret the scripture, only that sincerity and intelligent responsibility must complement one another. Ultimately, mature scriptural guidance comes from continual saturation of oneself with the principles and themes of the Bible as mediated through its concrete stories, histories, and letters.

With respect to using the scriptures as a resource for Christian theological thought, similar reminders are in order. To pick and choose amongst the scripture, skipping from book to book and passage to passage, as if the Bible were a complicated but totally consistent, deductive theological system is to do violence to the very manner in which the Bible was put together. The concrete, incarnational nature of biblical literature clearly entails that the scriptures are not a theological textbook full of direct and unambiguous truth. Rather, they are an indirect mediator of God's own incarnational, and thus mediated, self-revelation. As a repository of mediated truth, the scriptures must be interpreted historically and literarily without expecting to find its theological implications consistent at all points. Their mediated character requires that we distinguish between historical, experiential revelation in <u>event</u> and systematic, human theological interpretation in ideas.

Within the general interpretive principles thus outlined the Bible can, has, and does serve as powerful resource for everyday life and theological thinking. It stands in a triangular relationship with the historic and present Christian community on the one hand and the individual Christian's experience on the other. The three interpret one another; none is supreme over the others. This "check and balance" system does not

guarantee agreement, let alone absolute truth,
but it does provide an adequate basis for faith
and for doing God's work in the world.

One final word. There are those who interpret Paul's statement that "All scripture is inspired of God..." (2 Tim. 3:16) to entail biblical inerrancy. They claim that since the Greek
work translated "inspired" literally means "God-
breathed" (theopneustos), the bible cannot con-
tain any errors. Aside from such facts as Adam
and Eve's having been God-breathed and the church's
being Christ's body not keeping them from error
(and aside from the fact that inerrancy could only
be said to apply to the original manuscripts, all
of which the Christian community has never posses-
ed), this interpretation is not based on a thorough
reading of the passage in question.

In the previous verse (2 Tim. 3:15), Paul refers to the "sacred writings" with which Timothy
has been familiar as a child, and which were able
to make him "wise unto salvation." It is clear
from historical and biblical research that these
writings, the same ones Paul says are inspired of
God in verse sixteen, could only have been copies
of the Greek translation (the Septuigint) of the
Old Testament. So, whatever God-breathed means,
it must also apply to copies and translations of
the scripture -- and I cannot think of anyone who
would claim inerrancy for these. Besides, one
must believe in the authority of the scriptures
in a general and sufficient sense in order to pay
attention to what it says about itself in the
first place. Inerrancy is neither possible nor
necessary.

Chapter Fourteen

Kingdom Come: Here and Now, There and Then

The position which seems to me most consistent, with respect to understanding the nature
of the kingdom of God, is usually labeled "Amil-
lenariansim". Strictly speaking this term means
"no millenium", but it is used to designate that
view which stands opposed to any concept of the
rule of Christ for a literal thousand years here
on earth. The positive thrust of this view is on
the proper interpretation of biblical references
to the millenium as a symbol of Christ's final
victory and God's creation of a new heaven and a
new earth. Moreover, this position insists that
the New Testament view of the Kingdom includes
both a present and a future aspect, that the
Kingdom is both here and now and will be culminated in the future and elsewhere.

Here again it is imperative that we begin
with the character of the Incarnation. By its
very nature, the presence of Christ in our world
is mediated, indirect. While being sufficiently
revealed for those who seek, it is not beyond being misunderstood by others. Now we know God
"through a glass, darkly", but then we shall know
God "face to face." The New Testament promises
a time when the full glory of Christ will be revealed. So too with Christ's kingdom. Now it is
present in a sufficient but mediated form, some-
day it will be fully and directly experienced.
This latter aspect is what is denied by the existentialist interpretation, "realized eschatology",
but only at the expense of doing violence to the
main fabric of the New Testament.

Christ's own teaching about the Kingdom emphasizes both its present and future dimensions.

111

He frequently stressed that the Kingdom is "at hand" and "within" (among) us. He likened it to seeds which have small and difficult to discern beginnings, but which grow into great and obvious realities. Along these same lines, Christ often foretold the "day" when he would come again, actualizing the present potential and making all things new. These two aspects of Christ's teaching must be taken together and do not mutually exclude one another. At the same time it is clear from the way Christ describes the final culmination of the Kingdom that it will not be the work of humans, that it cannot be equated with a period in human history on the earth as we presently know it. Rather, the finalization of the Kingdom will come from "beyond history", as the work of God bringing an end to the human story as such.

The heart of the present interpretation of the Kingdom theme lies in the proper understanding of the notion of God's Kingdom itself. In the first place, it is clear form Christ's teachings that he regards the Kingdom as quite distinct from Kingdoms of the world. Several times he explicitly states that his Kingdom is "not of this world", and he upbraids the disciples especially for not understanding this. In fact, Christ's primary point of correction of the standard Jewish interpretation of the coming of the Messiah focuses on their propensity for viewing it as a re-establishment of the socio-political, military-economic Kingdom of David. They failed to grasp the spiritual, non-literal character of the prophetic promises, but saw them as guarantees that the Messiah would actually rule over them as they, in turn, ruled over their enemies. It is well-established that Jesus constantly sought to disassociate himself from this interpretation of the concept of Messiah.

In the second place, careful attention to the Greek term that is so often translated "Kingdom" in the New Testament will reveal that it actually means "Kingship". Thus the emphasis is on the quality of leadership and not upon a quantitative Kingdom involving land, subjects, rules, enemies, and the like. The Kingdom of God involves the rule of Christ in the hearts and lives of humankind, a qualitative condition which begins in the present, though not so as to render Christians a distinct socio-political group, and which will be culminated in the new creation. Surely this qualitative condition is what Jesus meant by insisting that his Kingdom is "within" us. In principle it is not a physical thing, but rather it is a spiritual relationship.

As far as the details of the future fulfillment of the Kingdom of God are concerned, the scriptures are significantly silent. The highly symbolic passages in Daniel, Ezekial, and Revelation which are often taken to be descriptive of the final outcome of this present age and the ushering in of a literal Kingdom, must be understood as apocalyptic literature. Such literature was written to comfort and exhort believers who were being persecuted by hostile powers (Babylon and Rome), being a kind of coded message for the immediate situation whose meaning was clear to those involved. In no sense can these passages be taken as a literal description of the future development of the Kingdom. The scriptures are relatively silent about the future--except to assure us that there will be a new creation--because "sufficient unto the day is the evil thereof." I often think that if the energy so many put into trying to predict God's future activity were put to sharing the gospel of love, what a different world this would be! Christ himself denied knowing when the end shall come, saying "Only the Father knows."

With respect to understanding the present form of the Kingdom, it is important to keep in

113

mind Christ's parable of the wheat and tares. (weeds). When the disciples wanted to get busy separating the latter from the former, Christ replied that it pleased the Father for the two to grow together for the present and that when it was time to separate them God would see to it. Thus it is not our business to judge between one person or group and another, although it is our responsibility, in terms of practical decision-making, to discern where the Kingship of Christ is operative. Judging focuses on the other person's quality and fate, while discerning emphasizes our own need to be stewards of what God as given us. It is a subtle but crucial distinction. God alone can act as Judge, and Jesus said there will be many surprises. (Matt. 25). We can only seek to follow the spirit of Christ vis à vis our own commitments.

A word here about rewards and punishments. Far too often people speak of the Gospel and of the Kingdom as if they are related in a means-end fashion, the former providing the "ticket", as it were, whereby "we get to go to heaven." Thus it frequently sounds as if being in a loving, faithful relationship with God is a means of "being saved" or living forever in heaven. As I understand the New Testament, being in a loving, faithful relationship with God, believing the Gospel, is an end-in-itself--it is heaven. God is not our means of avoiding pain and judgment and obtaining peace and joy, anymore than loving a friend or mate is a means of achieving happiness. Being in a loving relationship, whether with another human or with God, is its own reward.

Frankly, I think that the whole rewards and punishments motif is out of place in the Christian life, whether in this life or the next. This is what Jesus meant when he said "the first shall be last and the last shall be first", for to simply reverse the order of things, putting different people at the top, does not do justice to the radical character of the suffering servant ethic. I think Christ was saying, as he said with respect to how many times one should forgive another (70 times 7) and as to whether he came to call "sinners" or the "righteous" (all are sinners), that the whole business of making distinctions among people as to their worth and rank is simply set aside in the Kingdom.

The process of discerning what aspects and dimensions of our contemporary world are reflecting the spirit of Christ is as difficult as it is important. There is a variety of approaches which have been taken to this task within the Christian community past and present. For convenience sake they can be arranged on a continuum ranging from right to left, from "conservative" to "liberal". A brief examination of this continuum will help reveal some of the important factors involved in this crucial aspect of understanding the meaning of the Kingdom of God in our time. I shall borrow a typology from H.R. Niebuhr's insightful and influential book, Christ and Culture.

Early in the history of the Christian community, in a time of persecution, many thinkers took a pessimistic approach to the relationship between the Kingdom and the world. Tertullian, an important church father, asked rhetorically, "What has Athens to do with Jerusalem?", thereby implying that the world and God's Kingdom are essentially distinct and even opposed. This view has been revived from time to time through the ages (it was an important part of the rise of monasticism), and in our own day certain fundamentalists have urged that Christians separate themselves from "the world" and stand opposed to the principles and concerns of contemporary culture. This posture seems to ignore Christ's teaching on not judging between the wheat and the tares. Further, it is clearly non-incarnational in its effort to

115

keep Christianity separated from human error and
need.

In our own time the opposite extreme has
been frequently expressed by those taking an optimistic approach to the relation of the Kingdom
to the world. The liberal or "social gospel"
interpretation of Christianity has affirmed the
essential identity of God's Kingdom with human
progress. This view, which was the dominant one
during the last half of the 19th century, due to
the influence of the theory of evolution, fell on
hard times during the first half of the 20th century with its world wars, depression and the in-
vention of "the bomb". In recent years, however,
it has experienced a revival, partly as a result
of the counter-culture, "greening of America"
syndrome, but mostly because of the confidence
being placed in the social sciences. The belief
is that soon we shall be able to control and plan
our destiny, even in the face of our great ecological crisis. This approach fails to take adequate
account of the profundity of human limitation and
evil, and it ignores the New Testament emphasis
on the culmination of the Kingdom comimg from
"beyond history". Thus it largely undercuts the
possibility of a Christian prophetic critique of
contemporary society.

In between these two extremes stand two
other views which are more sophisticated in their
outlook. One is the Roman Catholic position which
acknowledges two Kingdoms, that of Christ and that
of the world, existing side by side. Both are from
God and thus they cannot be in conflict, but the
former takes precedence over the latter when they
appear to be in conflict. This hierarchy stands
opposed to the separation of church and state,
and has led to many conflicts between the two,
ranging from the Inquisition to opposition to
birth control. The other view, more closely af-
filiated with Lutheran theology, emphasizes the

116

two Kingdoms as standing side by side with each Christian a citizen of both, even though in many ways they conflict. Thus the Christian is confronted with a paradox and necessarily lives in tension between the demands of both Kingdoms. The Roman Catholic posture fails to do justice to the incarnational basis of the Kingdom of God, and it also confuses spiritual power with political power. The Lutheran posture seems both more realistic and biblical, but there is one important element missing.

The missing factor focuses what might be termed yet another approach. The incarnational nature of the Kingdom demands not only that it not be separated from nor identified with human culture on the one hand, nor that it rule over or exist merely side by side with it on the other hand. Rather, it demands as well that it seek to transform human culture by the reconciling power of God in Christ. To relate incarnationally with human culture is to interact with it in a redemptive way; indwelling it, loving it, and yet in such a way as to allow it its own freedom and development. This mediated transformation strikes me as the most properly Christian approach to the task of discerning God's Kingdom in the world today. One seeks the reconciling spirit of Christ in all activities and plans, being constantly open to finding him active in new and unexpected ways and places. In this way we can be in the world--fully involved and vulnerable servants--while still not being of the world--conformed to its system of values.

This concludes my brief introduction to what I have called an organic exploration of Christian theology. I have sought to center this exploration around a fresh and radical consideration of the notions of Incarnation and Atonement. The aim has been to trace out the ramifications of these notions for the other main Christian theological themes. My hope is that the initial survey of issues and positions in Part One, together with the perspective and suggestions of Part Two, will stimulate the reader to continue on his or her own pilgrimage Toward Theology.